THE
MARTINI
FIELD GUIDE

MARTINI CULTURE FOR THE
COCKTAIL RENAISSANCE

SHANE CARLEY

CIDER MILL PRESS

BOOK PUBLISHERS

This book can be ordered by mail from the publisher. Please include $5.99 for postage and handling. Please support your local bookseller first!

Books published by Cider Mill Press Book Publishers are available at special discounts for bulk purchases in the United States by corporations, institutions, and other organizations. For more information, please contact the publisher.

Cider Mill Press Book Publishers
"Where good books are ready for press"
501 Nelson Place
Nashville, Tennessee 37214
cidermillpress.com

Typography: Sackers Gothic, Mrs. Eaves, Freight Text, Freight Sans
Photo credits: page 194

Printed in Malaysia

23 24 25 26 27 COS 7 6 5 4 3

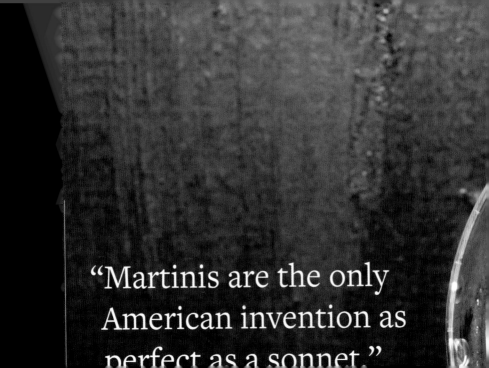

"Martinis are the only
American invention as
perfect as a sonnet."

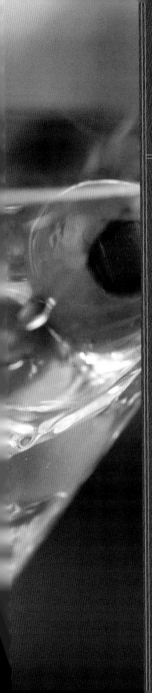

✦ CONTENTS ✦

INTRODUCTION

"The proper union of gin and vermouth
is a great and sudden glory; it is one
of the happiest marriages on earth,
and one of the shortest lived."
—Bernard DeVoto, American historian

COCKTAILS ARE NOT COMPLICATED. Literally anyone can create one—and spirit-slinging establishments of all kinds festoon their menus with new ones on a daily basis. Walk into just about any bar or restaurant in America and you'll find a bevy of specialty cocktails, often named for local celebrities or peppered with puns. Some are good. Some are bad. Very few have staying power. They are disposable recipes, designed to be purchased, enjoyed, and summarily forgotten.

What, then, makes a cocktail stand out? What elevates it to exalted status? What allows it to stand the test of time?

Enter the martini.

The classic martini is an astounding alchemy of gin and vermouth. It dates back to at least 1888, when the name was first used in *Harry Johnson's New and Improved Bartender's Manual*, and it remains one of the world's most popular cocktails. Simple, elegant, and flavorful, a traditional martini has just two ingredients and can be enjoyed by both cocktail aficionados and the uninitiated. Easy to mix, the cocktail requires no special tools or expertise to create. Beautiful to look at, it lends an air of class to any occasion. And delicious to drink, it allows even novice drinkers to understand that a careful balance of flavors can create something that is more than the sum of its parts.

We are living through a cocktail renaissance, and the martini is a special drink—one that deserves to be celebrated. *The Martini Field Guide* examines the iconic drink's history, its cultural impact, and its many different forms. With small-batch distilleries and bespoke cocktail joints popping up all over the globe, find out why James Bond's drink of choice will always find new fans.

→ 1 ←

THE HISTORY OF THE MARTINI

H. L. MENCKEN ONCE CALLED THE MARTINI "the only American invention as perfect as the sonnet." High praise from a man legendary for his exacting prose, and a sentiment that echoes throughout the acclaim that has been heaped on this cocktail for over 100 years.

The origin of the martini is difficult to pin down. The name "martini" is believed to derive from a brand of Italian vermouth named after its founder, Alessandro Martini. Some theories speculate that the cocktail was created by a bartender in Martinez, California, while others hypothesize that it simply adopted the name after becoming well known there. One popular theory even states that the drink originated when a miner during the California Gold Rush requested that a bartender create a brand-new cocktail to celebrate his striking it rich. Whether any version is true is up for debate, but the "Martinez Cocktail" does have several elements in common with the martini, and has been documented as far back as 1887—one year before *Harry Johnson's New and Improved Bartender's Manual* first applied the martini name to this iconic drink.

In truth, the true origin of the martini is lost to history, and connoisseurs of the cocktail are each likely to have a favorite pet theory. Perhaps you're among those who believe that the drink was first created in New York's Knickerbocker Hotel. Or perhaps you prefer the British theory that it was named for the Martini & Henry rifle, as the strength of the cocktail mimicked the gun's infamous kick. Countless cities, hotels, publications, and individuals have clamored to take credit for the original martini cocktail, and each theory has its own merits.

Whatever its origins, the martini became wildly popular in the 1920s, and during that time it settled into a more consistent and recognizable form: gin and vermouth, in a ratio nearing 2:1 or 3:1. The drink was known for being served at the aforementioned Knickerbocker Hotel, a favorite haunt of industrialists like John D. Rockefeller. As Rockefeller

and other public figures made their love of the cocktail known, it began to soar in popularity.

Of course, James Bond is likely more responsible for the martini's current popularity than any living, breathing individual. The beloved fictional spy, known for his suave demeanor, cool attitude, and hard-drinking lifestyle was known to Ian Fleming's readers as a martini lover. Published in 1953, Fleming's first novel, *Casino Royale*, features 007 famously ordering a Vesper Martini with very specific instructions: "Three measures of Gordon's, one of vodka, half a measure of Kina Lillet. Shake it very well until it's ice-cold, then add a large thin slice of lemon peel." But it wasn't until Sean Connery delivered the famous "shaken, not stirred" line in the film *Dr. No* that the mantra became ingrained in the minds of the general public. Since then, the request has appeared in a majority of Bond films, and was named one of the 100 Best Movie Quotes of the past 100 years by the American Film Institute, an honor that underscores the cultural relevance of the famous secret agent's drink order.

Since its rise to prominence, the martini has enjoyed the ebbs and flows of popularity that any fad must endure; however, the simplicity of the cocktail, and its ample opportunities for improvisation, ensure its periodic returns to trendiness. More than a drink, the martini serves as the perfect metaphor for America, the country in which it was almost certainly born: the martini is elegant, malleable, and strong. Perhaps David Wondrich of Liquor.com puts it best: "As things stand, the Martini is another American legend, like Billy the Kid: a larger-than-life invention of the nation's collective will."

Morning Glory Cocktail.

(Use medium bar-glass.)

Take 3 dashes of gum syrup.
  2 dashes of Curaçoa.
  2 dashes of Boker's bitters.
  1 dash of Absinthe.
  1 pony of brandy.
  1 pony of whiskey.
  1 piece of lemon peel, twisted to express the oil.
  2 small pieces of ice.

Stir thoroughly and remove the ice. Fill the glass with Seltzer water or plain soda, and stir with a teaspoon having a little sugar in it.

Martinez Cocktail.

(Use small bar-glass.)

Take 1 dash of Boker's bitters.
  2 dashes of Maraschino.
  1 pony of Old Tom gin.
  1 wine-glass of Vermouth.
  2 small lumps of ice.

Shake up thoroughly, and strain into a large cocktail glass. Put a quarter of a slice of lemon in the glass, and serve. If the guest prefers it very sweet, add two dashes of gum syrup.

Recipe for the Martinez Cocktail, predecessor to the martini, from *The Bar-tender's Guide; or How to Mix All Kinds of Plain and Fancy Drinks* by Jerry Thomas.

2

THE HISTORY
OF GIN

Illustration from the book *The Newe* [*sic*] *Jewell of Health* by Conrad Gesner (1576).

THE HISTORY OF GIN IS NEARLY as muddled as that of the martini. Although popular culture credits Franciscus Sylvius, a physician from the Netherlands, with creating the beverage in the 1600s, gin (or its clear precursor) has been recorded as far back as the 1200s.

First mentioned in an early encyclopedia known as the *Der Naturen Bloeme*, "genever" was the predecessor to what we today know as gin. Still popular in certain parts of the world (including the Netherlands), genever is a juniper-flavored beverage that shares many elements with its better-known contemporary. Genever was the drink of choice in the Dutch military in the late 1500s, and some believe that the term "Dutch courage" refers to the beverage being used to embolden soldiers before battle.

Gin began its rise to prominence in the 17th century as the Dutch became increasingly powerful on the world stage. William of Orange is credited with popularizing the drink in Great Britain, as Dutch gin was imported in much greater quantities during his occupation of England. Not surprisingly, the expansion of gin into new markets, and its steadily increasing popularity, led to new innovations in the distillation process, and gin began to slowly evolve into the form we recognize today.

The process of making gin is variable, depending on the type of still being used. Both genever and early gins were made using copper pot stills, in which a grain mash was distilled and redistilled with flavoring botanicals. Due in large part to the inefficiency of these early pot stills, genever and early iterations of gin were generally low in alcohol content.

(top) The boiler in a small Old Country gin distillery.
(bottom) Interior of ancient distillery in Schiedam, Netherlands, for producing the traditional genever.

The introduction of column stills in the early 1800s made the production of gin more efficient and potent. Essentially a series of small pot stills, column stills allow for continuous distillation—eliminating the need for "batches" of gin—while distilling a higher concentration of consumable alcohol. This allowed for the production of stronger gin in greater quantities than had been previously possible.

As different types of both pot and column stills have been developed, methods for infusing the flavor of these botanicals have varied—though the stills themselves are still copper in all but the rarest cases. Distillers may prefer to use different stills depending on their preferred flavoring methods. Hendrick's, for instance, uses both the "Carter-Head" still—known for its long neck and vapor-driven infusion method—and the "Bennett" still—a small pot still that is rarely seen today but is famous for imparting robust flavors.

Today, many gins start with a neutral (flavorless) alcohol and add botanicals afterward, rather than the grain mash method used during gin's early days. Other gin producers elect to infuse their gin with essential oils, a method that allows for more affordable production, but is generally viewed as being less refined. Although the primary flavoring agent in gin will always be juniper, different gin makers have chosen to emphasize flavors that range from floral to herbal, offering drinkers a range of styles and flavor options—a variability that is reflected in the wide range of gins available today.

As is typical of many alcoholic beverages, gin consumption grew as regulations governing the production of alcohol were eased. Because gin could be produced with lower-quality barley than necessary to produce beer, it quickly gained popularity as an affordable alternative to other types of alcohol. This rapid rise in popularity, which occurred during the first half of the 18th century, would eventually become known as the

"Gin Craze," and the glut of cheap gin available meant that it was accessible to even the poorest members of society. This accessibility led to a stigmatization of gin that has, in some form, lasted to this day, with phrases like "gin mill" and "gin joint" retaining negative connotations.

The centuries since the Gin Craze have been quieter, but the gin market has evolved considerably. At different times, changing regulations have led to the popularization of sweeter gins, dryer gins, more herbal gins, and other slight variations on the juniper theme. Many of these styles survive today, such as "London Dry" gin. This, the most popular style of gin, lacks the sweetness of other offerings and is usually high in alcohol content. London Dry gin is also known for the inclusion of citrus peel among its botanicals, an element often detectable in its aroma.

Today, you can walk into any liquor store in America and find an entire wall dedicated to gin. It's a testament not just to its staying power, but also to the martini's—a cocktail that can endure the ups and downs of its most important ingredient and remain a cultural staple the world over.

A London gin palace, 1850.

dried juniper berries

hibiscus flower

lavender

coriander

cinchona bark (quinine)

sarsaparilla

cardamom

jasmine

sloe berries

citrus peels

cassia bark

elderflower

beach plums

orris root

→ 3 ←

THE HISTORY
OF VERMOUTH

> "I would like to observe the vermouth from across the room while I drink my martini."
>
> WINSTON CHURCHILL

GIN DATES BACK CENTURIES, but vermouth dates back millennia. Fortified wines were being prepared in China prior to 1000 BCE, and these are the earliest predecessors of what we now call vermouth. Among the earliest herbal additions to these wines was wormwood, a bitter herb known in Germany as *wermut*, and from which vermouth takes its name.

By sheer coincidence, vermouth rose to prominence in Europe around the same time as gin. "Wormwood wines" from Italy, Germany, and France became increasingly popular, and the sweet and dry forms of vermouth began to take shape. Italy is generally considered to be the first country to produce vermouth in its current form, and it was in Turin, Italy, that the beverage was first popularized as an aperitif rather than a medicinal tonic.

Turin's Antonio Benedetto Carpano is generally considered the first to commercialize the modern form of the drink, and it wasn't long before other vermouth makers began to appear in the region—including Martini & Rossi, which still exists today. Indeed, many of today's best known vermouth makers are Italian. The renaissance of vermouth makers in Turin quickly brought the spirit to prominence, and by the 1700s the drink was readily available as far away as England.

Although the red color of sweet vermouth and the clear color of dry vermouth might lead the uninitiated to believe that red and white wines, respectively, are used to create each concoction, the truth is that both the sweet and dry versions contain a similar wine base. Sweet vermouth takes on a reddish-brown hue from the caramel that is added. If red and white wines were the basis for sweet and dry vermouth, respectively, their colors would likely be reversed, since it is red wine that is typically considered "dry" and white wine that is considered "sweet."

Following vermouth's transition from medicinal liquor to popular aperitif, it wasn't long before it began appearing in cocktails. From there, its inclusion in the martini was right around the corner.

Today, vermouth is rarely consumed by itself, at least in the United States. Instead, it is used primarily as a flavoring agent in cocktails such as the martini, the Manhattan, and the Negroni, as it provides the perfect accent for a number of spirits.

Cocktails with Vermouth

Dry Martini

Negroni

Manhattan

Vermouth Royale

Rose

Old Pal

Vodka Martini

Rob Roy

Martinez

Bronx

Gibson

Tuxedo

Americano

Adonis

Bijou

Bitter Orange

Bloodhound

Dirty Martini

Boulevardier

Blood and Sand

Vermouth and Tonic

→ 4 ←

SHAKEN OR
STIRRED?

> "Martinis should always be stirred, not shaken, so that the molecules lie sensuously on top of one another."
>
> W. SOMERSET MAUGHAM

JAMES BOND'S PREFERENCE for a shaken martini is well known, but the debate over whether the cocktail is better mixed by shaking or stirring is far from settled. Bartenders, martini lovers, and even biochemists have weighed in over the years, each approaching the debate from a different angle.

When the martini first rose to prominence, stirring was the prescribed mixing method. This fact alone leads many martini lovers to adhere to the rule, as they believe the stirred version to be the drink's purest form. Others subscribe to the belief that shaking gin "bruises" the liquor, leaving it with a more bitter taste.

Some have speculated that 007's love of shaken martinis derives from the fact that certain vodkas are made from potato rather than grain, giving them an oily quality. A shaken martini is, anecdotally at least, better at dispersing the oil, which results in a smoother drink. Shaking also appears to incorporate the vermouth, which may also have a slightly oily quality, more thoroughly.

Of course, there is much more to the debate than the texture of the alcohol or the proper way to chill it. Scientists have even entered the fray, conducting studies, performing research, and identifying empirical, quantifiable differences between the shaken and stirred martini.

John Hayes, a food science professor at Penn State University, once told NPR that shaking a martini dilutes the drink, giving it a more watery quality. Unlike stirring, shaking a cocktail chips away at the ice, resulting in tiny flakes that melt as the drink warms. On the other hand, these tiny ice flakes help keep the drink cold for a longer period of time.

Hayes went on to speculate that Bond's preference for this slight dilution of the cocktail might be because it kept his head clearer, giving him a mental edge in the risky situations in which he typically found himself. However, not everyone is this generous in their interpretation. President Bartlet, of *The West Wing* fame, once said of his fictional counterpart, "shaken, not stirred, will get you cold water with a dash of gin and dry vermouth. The reason you stir it with a special spoon is so not to chip the ice. James is ordering a weak martini and being snooty about it."

In 1999, a team of biochemists at the University of Western Ontario conducted their own study of the difference between shaken and stirred martinis. They discovered that a shaken martini contains slightly more antioxidants than a stirred martini, although they were unable to determine what caused the disparity.

Whether antioxidants actually affect the taste of a martini is a separate debate, but one chemist who participated in the study has continued researching other elements that impact the flavor of the cocktail. Darcy O'Neil agrees with the theory that potato vodka has an oily quality, and confirms that his tests indicate that shaking a martini made with potato vodka successfully dissipates that oil. He also agrees that shaking a martini will make it colder, but notes that after 20 shakes or so, a cocktail has generally gotten as cold as it's going to get.

Boston-based culinary scientist Dave Arnold has thoughts of his own on the matter. While he agrees with O'Neil that shaking a cocktail will make it colder, he points out that the ability to detect certain flavors is impeded when a drink becomes too cold. Sweetness, in particular, becomes more difficult to taste, and Arnold recommends adding additional sweetener to a drink if you plan to shake it.

If you've ever shaken a drink yourself, chances are you've encountered Arnold's next talking point: air bubbles. Egg whites are a common cocktail ingredient because, when shaken, the bubbles they generate create a beautiful foamy texture. The martini lacks an ingredient that reacts this way, and the air bubbles generated by shaking it dissipate extremely quickly. Because of this, Arnold recommends making a smaller drink if you plan to shake it, so that you can consume it before the bubbles disappear, as they add a unique texture that should not be wasted.

So, what's the verdict?

Those in search of a classic martini experience should order their drink stirred. Those who would like to be sure that the gin (or vodka) and vermouth are mixed as thoroughly as possible should order their drink shaken. Those looking for a colder martini should shake it. Those looking for a sweeter martini should stir it. In the end, the two methods produce different results, but which version is "better" is determined entirely by personal preference.

Try both versions and decide for yourself!

5

TOOLS OF THE TRADE AND GARNISHES

TOOLS OF THE TRADE

MIXING A MARTINI ISN'T COMPLICATED, but there are a few tools that will make it easier. A cocktail stirrer will help you mix a classic martini with little frustration. A cocktail shaker will help you prepare a Bradford Martini without making a mess. A strainer will help you make just about any cocktail.

While these tools are not essential, they are undeniably helpful, and this section will provide additional insight into their many uses.

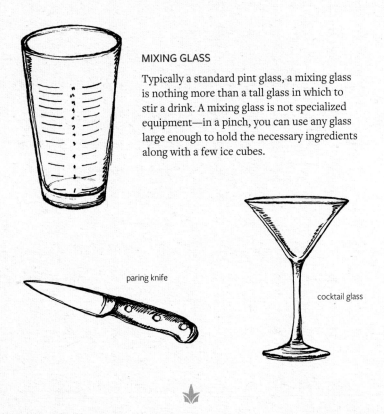

MIXING GLASS

Typically a standard pint glass, a mixing glass is nothing more than a tall glass in which to stir a drink. A mixing glass is not specialized equipment—in a pinch, you can use any glass large enough to hold the necessary ingredients along with a few ice cubes.

paring knife

cocktail glass

JIGGER

A jigger is just a fancy name for the most common measuring tool in a mixologist's arsenal. Shaped like a shot glass (and with approximately the same capacity, a jigger allows you to quickly and easily measure either "parts" or ounces.

highball glass

bottle for bitters

bar towels

COCKTAIL SHAKER

A cocktail shaker is a container about the size of a pint glass, usually made from metal, with a screw top. The shaker provides a simple way to mix a cocktail, both combining the necessary ingredients and chilling them with ice. A basic cocktail shaker is relatively inexpensive, and you are better off purchasing this specific tool than trying to jury-rig a shaker for yourself.

rocks glass

champagne flute

STRAINER

Used in tandem with either a mixing glass or cocktail shaker, the strainer simply strains the cocktail after it has been mixed. This keeps the ice cubes (in the case of a mixing glass) or broken ice chips (in the case of a cocktail shaker) out of your drink. Because ice waters down a drink when it melts, the strainer is an important tool for keeping your cocktail pure.

MUDDLER

Similar to a pestle, this simple tool is used to mash (muddle) ingredients such as fruits or herbs. Muddling fruits releases the juice within, adding a fresh quality to a drink, while muddling certain herbs helps activate their flavors. A simple muddler can often be found on the top end of a cocktail shaker, though fancier, specialized muddlers are available for minimal cost.

shot glass

coupe

COCKTAIL STIRRER

There are plenty of fancy cocktail stirrers, but most take the form of a small spoon with a long handle. Used in conjunction with a mixing glass, the purpose of the cocktail stirrer is exactly as it sounds: to quickly and easily stir any cocktail. If you don't have a designated cocktail stirrer, you can use any spoon—you just may find it more difficult to navigate the ice cubes.

GARNISHES

GARNISHES MAY SEEM LIKE THE least important part of a cocktail, but the truth is that they can fundamentally change the drink. For a drink like the martini, the simple splash of color added by an olive or a maraschino cherry can alter the way the cocktail is perceived. It is often said that "you eat with your eyes first," and drinking cocktails follows the same rule.

Not only are garnishes pleasing to the eye, they are often also pleasing to the palate. Olives, cherries, cocktail onions, pickles, and other delicious treats can often be found accompanying cocktails—the martini in particular. Other garnishes that are not eaten, like the lemon or lime twist, can still impart flavor and add an element of beauty to the drink.

Carefully consider your garnish when making a martini. Olives will impart a salty quality, while blue cheese will add richness. A lemon twist will add a hint of citrus, while a cornichon will impart both sweet and sour flavors to the cocktail. Which one you choose depends on your personal taste.

CITRUS TWIST

A lemon or lime twist can often be found in a martini, and is nothing more than a long strip of peel that has been twisted to lend it a curly look. As both lemon and lime peels tend to hold their shape easily after they have been curled, they are the go-to options when a citrus twist is called for.

Although citrus rinds are not generally eaten, they do retain some of their fruit's flavor, imparting a subtle hint of citrus to a cocktail. The oil from the outside of the peel can also be used to coat the edge of a cocktail glass, adding another hint of both flavor and aroma to the drink.

You are unlikely to find citrus twists sold at a grocery or liquor store, so making your own will be necessary. A simple knife will do the trick once the rind has been peeled, or you can use a channeling knife to slice around the entire lemon or lime.

"Happiness is finding two olives in your Martini when you're hungry."

JOHNNY CARSON

PIMENTO OLIVE

Olives are the most common garnish for the martini, and they come in many forms. The pimento-stuffed olive is the version you're most likely to see, largely because they are the version most commonly found in your average grocery store.

Pimentos (also known as cherry peppers) are small, red, and mild. As a result, they don't add much more to the olive than color, though you may occasionally see olives stuffed with larger pimentos, which imparts a bit more flavor.

While you can find pimento-stuffed olives in any grocery store, you can also make them yourself, by purchasing some olives in brine and stuffing them with pimentos of your desired size.

CITRUS OLIVE

The citrus olive is less common than the pimento olive and consists of olives brined and stuffed with lemon peel. The lemon peel adds both sour and bitter elements, and although you might not normally think of eating lemon rind, it can impart a welcome hint of flavor when prepared by a deft hand.

You won't find citrus olives in many grocery stores, so you will likely have to make them. You can do this by thinly slicing lemon peel and inserting it into individual olives. You may want to use larger olives for this task, and may also find it helpful to make an x-shaped incision at the top of the olive to make the stuffing process easier. You should allow the citrus olives to steep in the brine for a few days before consumption, so that the lemon rind has time to soften.

Citrus olives combine the salty, briny elements of the olive with the bitter and sour elements of the lemon rind, creating a garnish perfect for both gin- and vodka-based martinis.

BLUE CHEESE OLIVE

Blue cheese olives are fairly common, though their use is limited mainly to the Dirty Martini or Filthy Martini. The richness of blue cheese makes it an ingredient best used sparingly, but when appropriate it can add a nice, creamy element to the typically sharp flavor of the martini.

You can find blue cheese-stuffed olives in most grocery stores, but discerning cheese lovers may want to make them with their own preferred style of this cheese that can range from creamy to pungent. Although painstaking, the process is not difficult, and requires little more than a cheese knife and a bit of patience. Simply place your favorite blue cheese crumbles in the opening of an olive. Consume immediately or allow them to steep in brine.

Although blue cheese olives go best with the aforementioned Dirty or Filthy Martinis, feel free to experiment by adding them to any variation you like (though it is recommended you keep them away from any cocktail involving sweet vermouth).

MARASCHINO CHERRY

One of the most popular drink garnishes is the maraschino cherry, a sweet, sugary, and alarmingly red cherry that lends a candy-like quality to any drink it appears in. Typically made from sweet cherries sugared within an inch of their lives, maraschino cherries are the ultimate guilty pleasure garnish.

Maraschino cherries are common, but if you wish to avoid the slightly medicinal flavor of the syrup in which they are generally preserved, you can make your own at home. To do so, create a homemade simple syrup by mixing equal parts sugar and water and heating until the sugar dissolves. Add a small hint of vanilla extract, stir it in, and let it cool.

Next, place pitted cherries in a mason jar and add the simple syrup until the cherries are covered. Then, store the jar in the fridge for a few days to allow the flavor to set in. Once a bit of time has passed, you'll have a deliciously fresh version of one of the most popular cocktail garnishes.

COCKTAIL ONION

You could certainly be forgiven for thinking that adding an onion to a cocktail is a terrible idea. And if we were talking about a traditional onion, you would be correct. It's unlikely that any bar will be racing to add sliced onion to a cocktail anytime soon (well, other than a Bloody Mary).

A cocktail onion is a little bit different. They are traditionally made from pearl onions that have been soaked in brine along with a bit of sugar and spice. Because pearl onions are naturally sweet, they avoid the overly aromatic, eye-watering element that most people associate with raw onions.

You can find cocktail onions in most grocery stores, but you can also make your own by soaking pearl onions in a salty brine. Some recipes call for a hint of turmeric or paprika, while others call for adding dry vermouth to the brine. If you intend to use cocktail onions as a garnish for martinis, you may want to heed this last bit of advice.

Cocktail onions make a delicious garnish for just about any martini variation. In fact, some believe that they change the drink so much that they gave a martini garnished with a cocktail onion its own name: the Gibson.

PICKLED PEPPER

Pickled peppers can take many forms. Popular versions include jalapeños, banana peppers, red peppers, green peppers, and serrano peppers, though any pepper will do. Chances are, which pickled pepper you prefer depends on the level of heat your palate can tolerate.

When it comes to cocktail garnishes, pickled peppers occasionally make an appearance. This should come as no surprise, since pimento-stuffed olives are a common martini garnish. But, as with cocktail onions, the idea of garnishing a cocktail with a vegetable can sometimes take people aback.

Different pickled peppers complement different drinks. For instance, a pickled jalapeño (or even a jalapeño-stuffed olive) goes well with a Spicy Martini. The vinegary bite of a pickled banana pepper pairs well with the salty brine in a Dirty Martini. A pickled serrano pepper might properly accent a Rosemary Martini, and a pickled red pepper adds a touch of sweetness to any drink.

You can find pickled peppers of all varieties in most grocery stores, or you can make your own by briefly simmering them in vinegar, water, and garlic. After cooling, add both the peppers and simmering liquid to a mason jar and store in the fridge for a few days.

"I never go jogging. It makes me spill my martini."

GEORGE BURNS

CORNICHON

Although not the most common martini garnish, the salty, sour flavor of the cornichon is a nice addition to the Pickled Martini, the Spicy Martini, and several other variations.

Cornichons are a small, sweet variety of pickle often served with charcuterie. Mild in flavor with just a hint of sourness, they are the perfect accompaniment to a subtly flavored cocktail like the martini. Where other pickles might overwhelm the drink, cornichons accent it nicely, playing off the round flavor of the vermouth.

While you could certainly pickle your own cornichons at home, they are primarily found in their already-pickled form, making a DIY version more trouble than it's worth.

6

GIN MARTINIS
AND VARIATIONS

"One martini is alright. Two are too many, and three are not enough."

JAMES THURBER

GIN DRINKS

GIN IS THE BACKBONE of the martini. Its fundamental ingredient. Whether you prefer your martini dry or wet, with dry vermouth or sweet vermouth, shaken or stirred, every decision is made with gin in mind.

In a way, gin itself is a reflection of the martini. It's simple, yet flavorful. The juniper is omnipresent, accented in small ways by different distillers, but providing a fundamental flavor profile that sets it apart from other liquors. Like the martini, gin can be an acquired taste, but those who enjoy it tend to love it.

With that in mind, these classic martini recipes paint a picture of a devoted audience. There are many different ways to envision the martini, and many different ways to enjoy it. But traditional martinis stray little from the recipe that has endured since the turn of the century.

Sample one recipe or sample them all. Choose your favorite or create something new. The martini is revered for its simplicity, but also appreciated for its adaptability. The true beauty of the martini lies in the fact that the perfect martini rests in the eye of the beholder.

CLASSIC MARTINI

If you want a traditional experience, turn to the Classic Martini. Simple, elegant, and easy to mix, the Classic Martini is the most straightforward version of the cocktail, accessible to all and offering the same great flavors experienced by the drink's earliest devotees. The Classic Martini is crisp, clean, and delicious.

INGREDIENTS:

4 parts Tanqueray gin
1 part dry vermouth
1 lemon twist, for garnish

DIRECTIONS:

1. Add the gin and vermouth to a mixing glass filled with ice.
2. Stir until thoroughly mixed.
3. Strain the resulting mixture into a cocktail glass.
4. Garnish with a twist of lemon.

HIGHBROW MARTINI

Those looking to elevate their experience may turn to the Highbrow Martini. Bombay Sapphire gin is infused with 10 different flavor elements, including almond, lemon peel, licorice, and coriander. Although you may not be able to identify these elements individually, together they add a welcome depth of flavor to the gin. Used in a martini, Bombay Sapphire creates a unique and luxurious drinking experience.

INGREDIENTS:

4 parts Bombay Sapphire gin
1 part dry vermouth
1 lemon twist, for garnish

DIRECTIONS:

1. Add the gin and vermouth to a mixing glass filled with ice.
2. Stir until thoroughly mixed.
3. Strain the resulting mixture into a cocktail glass.
4. Garnish with a twist of lemon.

BUDGET MARTINI

One of the wonderful things about gin is that, unlike many other liquors, there are high-quality products available for budget prices. New Amsterdam gin is not expensive, but you might be surprised at the quality. Fans of New Amsterdam will tell you that there is little reason to spring for more expensive gin, and, after mixing up a Budget Martini, you might just find yourself agreeing with them.

INGREDIENTS:

4 parts New Amsterdam gin
1 part dry vermouth
1 dash lemon juice

DIRECTIONS:

1. Add the gin, vermouth, and lemon juice to a mixing glass filled with ice.
2. Stir until thoroughly mixed.
3. Strain the resulting mixture into a cocktail glass.

BRADFORD MARTINI

What separates the Bradford Martini from its standard cousin? As far as its ingredients, nothing. The Bradford is simply the name occasionally applied to a martini that is mixed by shaking rather than stirring. Although the terms are infrequently used today, the stirred martini has occasionally been referenced as the "Marguerite," while the shaken version is called the "Bradford." For an examination of the benefits of shaking or stirring, read the "Shaken or Stirred?" section of this book.

INGREDIENTS:

4 parts gin
1 part dry vermouth
1 lemon twist, for garnish

DIRECTIONS:

1. Add gin and vermouth to a cocktail shaker filled with ice.
2. Shake well.
3. Strain the resulting mixture into a cocktail glass.
4. Garnish with a twist of lemon.

"I think I had it in the back of my mind that I wanted to sound like a dry martini."

PAUL DESMOND, saxophone player

DRY MARTINI

What makes a Dry Martini dry? Why, the gin, of course. Colloquially, the higher the ratio of gin to vermouth, the drier the martini is said to be. The gin-to-vermouth ratio of a Dry Martini is likely to vary greatly depending on who you ask, with some sources pinning it as low as 3:1 and others as high as 15:1, 25:1, or even 100:1. As with most cocktails, the correct answer comes down to personal preference. For our purposes, a ratio double that of the Classic Martini will suffice.

INGREDIENTS:

8 parts gin
1 part dry vermouth
1 lemon twist, for garnish

DIRECTIONS:

1. Add the gin and vermouth to a mixing glass filled with ice.
2. Stir until thoroughly mixed.
3. Strain the resulting mixture into a cocktail glass.
4. Garnish with a twist of lemon.

How is it possible to measure a 100:1 ratio? The truth is, it isn't (unless you want to be highly scientific about it). When a drink is mixed at an absurdly high ratio such as 50:1 or 100:1, most bartenders or mixologists will simply use their best guess. To make a martini at a ratio of 100:1, simply add a small splash of vermouth to the gin. That approximation will do the trick.

PERFECT MARTINI

"Perfect" isn't just another differentiator, like the Highbrow Martini or the Budget Martini. The Perfect Martini specifically signifies a martini made with equal parts dry and sweet vermouth. If you didn't know there was a martini that makes use of sweet vermouth, you're probably not alone. It's a lesser-known variant, but it adds a welcome hint of sweetness to offset the crisp clarity of the standard version. Try it once and you just might start to swear by it.

INGREDIENTS:

5 parts gin
1 part dry vermouth
1 part sweet vermouth
1 lemon twist, for garnish

DIRECTIONS:

1. Add the gin and vermouths to a mixing glass filled with ice.
2. Stir until thoroughly mixed.
3. Strain the resulting mixture into a cocktail glass.
4. Garnish with a twist of lemon.

SWEET MARTINI

Where the Perfect Martini incorporates dry and sweet vermouth in equal parts, the Sweet Martini eschews the dry vermouth entirely in favor of a healthy dose of its more sugary cousin. Sweet vermouth not only lends this drink an entirely different flavor profile, but a darker, rosier complexion as well. The Sweet Martini pairs well with various fruit garnishes that would feel out of place with a more traditional martini, but complement the sweetness of this cocktail.

INGREDIENTS:

3 parts gin
1 part sweet vermouth
1 maraschino cherry, for garnish

DIRECTIONS:

1. Add the gin and vermouth to a mixing glass filled with ice.
2. Stir until thoroughly mixed.
3. Strain the resulting mixture into a cocktail glass.
4. Garnish with a maraschino cherry on a toothpick.

DIRTY MARTINI

When told that the Dirty Martini involves a splash of olive brine directly into the cocktail, some people react with disgust. Why introduce an ingredient that seems so unappetizing on its own? The truth is, while you may not want to drink olive brine on its own, the slight hint of vinegar and major dose of salt add a fascinating counterpoint to the bitter juniper flavor of the gin and the richness of the vermouth. Since many martini recipes call for an olive garnish, it shouldn't be a shock to see that flavor further incorporated, but trying it for yourself will make you a true believer.

INGREDIENTS:

4 parts gin
1 part dry vermouth
1 splash olive brine
3 pimento-stuffed olives, for garnish

DIRECTIONS:

1. Add the gin, vermouth, and olive brine to a mixing glass filled with ice.
2. Stir until thoroughly mixed.
3. Strain the resulting mixture into a cocktail glass.
4. Garnish with pimento-stuffed olives on a toothpick.

FILTHY MARTINI

One step up from the Dirty Martini is the Filthy Martini. The Filthy Martini takes the salty, briny goodness of the Dirty Martini and amps it up with a blue cheese-stuffed olive, and some blue cheese crumbles on top of the drink to boot. It might sound like a weird flavor combination, but it's one that has proven popular over the years.

INGREDIENTS:

4 parts gin
1 part dry vermouth
1 splash olive brine
3 blue cheese-stuffed olives, for garnish
1 handful blue cheese crumbles, for garnish

DIRECTIONS:

1. Add the gin, vermouth, and olive brine to a mixing glass filled with ice.
2. Stir until thoroughly mixed.
3. Strain the resulting mixture into a cocktail glass.
4. Crumble a small amount of blue cheese over the drink.
5. Garnish with blue cheese-stuffed olives on a toothpick.

VESPER MARTINI

The Vesper Martini was originally invented by James Bond (or rather, Ian Fleming, the man who created Bond). The drink, named in honor of the famous spy's one time lover Vesper Lynd, adds a splash of vodka and replaces the standard dry vermouth with a similar ingredient, Lillet. Although Fleming likely never intended for the cocktail to catch on, the Vesper Martini has taken on a life of its own, remaining popular to this day.

INGREDIENTS:

6 parts gin
2 parts vodka
1 part Lillet
1 slice lemon peel, for garnish

DIRECTIONS:

1. Add gin, vodka, and Lillet to a cocktail shaker filled with ice.
2. Shake well.
3. Strain the resulting mixture into a cocktail glass.
4. Garnish with a slice of lemon peel.

The Vesper Martini (or simply "Vesper") is ordered by James Bond in the novel *Casino Royale*, and never again after that. The drink does make an appearance in the movie adaptation of the novel, which features Daniel Craig in the role of the famous spy.

"I exercise strong self-control. I never drink anything stronger than gin before breakfast."

W. C. FIELDS

VARIATIONS ON GIN MARTINIS

Gin has such a distinct, specific flavor that many mixologists shy away from using it in cocktails. Indeed, you'll find that most cocktails involving gin are designed to accentuate the juniper flavor rather than hide it. This is part of what makes the martini such a special cocktail: it lets the gin stand on its own, offering only the slightest of nudges in one direction or another.

This isn't to say that gin cocktails can't incorporate a wide range of different flavors. In fact, the martini lends itself well to the subtle flavor variations that herbs, spices, liqueurs, bitters, and a number of other options can provide.

The key, as with all things, lies with both quality and quantity. A single well-placed mint sprig adds more to a martini than all the crème de menthe in the world. A dash of orange bitters will provide the zesty accent that even the freshest orange juice cannot. And a maraschino cherry infuses more sweetness and color than the best cherry liqueur money can buy.

In this section, you'll find a number of recipes for martini variants. Some will feature standard liqueurs. Others will feature more uncommon ingredients. But all of them have been thoughtfully crafted to perfectly complement the gin and vermouth flavors martini lovers adore.

ORANGE MARTINI

"Toothpaste and orange juice" is the go-to example of flavors that just don't mix. Why, then, is the Orange Martini so delicious? While the almost-minty flavor of the gin and the citrus elements of the orange don't seem like logical companions, the addition of orange bitters goes a long way in this cocktail. The bitters ground the drink, and using blood orange liqueur rather than the more common triple sec gives the cocktail a more rounded, almost savory element that enhances the gin and vermouth in ways you might not expect.

INGREDIENTS:

5 parts gin
1 part dry vermouth
1 part blood orange liqueur
1 dash orange bitters
1 orange twist, for garnish

DIRECTIONS:

1. Add the gin, vermouth, blood orange liqueur, and bitters to a cocktail shaker filled with ice.
2. Shake well.
3. Strain the resulting mixture into a cocktail glass.
4. Garnish with a twist of orange.

BREAKFAST MARTINI

The Breakfast Martini takes breakfast-y elements like orange juice and maple syrup and combines them into a delicious, welcoming cocktail. If you fall into the "stirred, not shaken" camp, you may wish to abandon your preference for this one: the maple syrup is a critical element, and shaking the cocktail well is the only way to ensure that it properly emulsifies.

INGREDIENTS:

2 parts gin
1 part triple sec
1 splash lemon juice
1 splash maple syrup

DIRECTIONS:

1. Pour the ingredients into a cocktail shaker filled with ice.
2. Shake well.
3. Strain the resulting mixture into a cocktail glass.

LIME MARTINI

Gin and lime are a time-honored combination. The classic gin-and-tonic cocktail is little more than gin, lime juice, and a bit of tonic water, so it only makes sense to offer up a lime-centric variant of the martini. The Lime Martini is as simple and elegant as the cocktail upon which it is based, adding just an extra splash of citrus to draw out the juniper. Give this cocktail an extra punch by taking some lime peel and rubbing the rim of the cocktail glass to impart added flavor.

INGREDIENTS:

4 parts gin
1 part dry vermouth
1 part lime juice
1 lime slice, for garnish

DIRECTIONS:

1. Add the gin, dry vermouth, and lime juice to a mixing glass filled with ice.
2. Stir thoroughly.
3. Take a bit of lime peel and rub it along the rim of a cocktail glass.
4. Strain the mixture from the cocktail shaker into the cocktail glass.
5. Garnish with a slice of lime.

MINT MARTINI

Perhaps more than anything else, the addition of fresh ingredients is guaranteed to raise the quality of a cocktail. Fresh orange brings out the flavor of triple sec. Fresh lime juice is far superior to concentrated versions. And you'll find that fresh herbs like mint can accompany spirits like gin shockingly well. The addition of crème de menthe and fresh mint add a refreshing quality to the juniper flavor of the gin and help create this delicious martini.

INGREDIENTS:

6 parts gin
1 part dry vermouth
1 part crème de menthe
3 fresh mint leaves, plus 3 more for garnish

DIRECTIONS:

1. At the bottom of a cocktail shaker, muddle the 3 mint leaves with the crème de menthe.
2. Add the gin and dry vermouth to the shaker.
3. Shake well.
4. Strain the resulting mixture into a cocktail glass.
5. Garnish with 3 fresh mint leaves.

CHRISTMAS MARTINI

The Christmas Martini is similar to the Mint Martini, but adds a festive element. A candy cane not only adds flavor to the cocktail, but a splash of color as well. This variation is perfect for Christmas dinner, a holiday party, or even just curling up in front of a warm fire.

INGREDIENTS:

3 parts gin
1 part dry vermouth
1 part peppermint schnapps
Candy cane crumbles, for the rim
1 peppermint, for garnish

DIRECTIONS:

1. Add gin, vermouth, and schnapps to a mixing glass filled with ice.
2. Stir thoroughly.
3. Wet the rim of the cocktail glass and then dip it into the crumbled candy cane.
3. Strain the contents of the cocktail shaker into the cocktail glass.
4. Garnish with a peppermint.

ROSEMARY MARTINI

Mint isn't the only herb that goes well with gin. A bit of fresh rosemary can also draw a bit more out of the liquor—particularly if you're using a high-quality gin like Bombay Sapphire. The inclusion of rosemary as both an ingredient and a garnish gives the drink not just a fresh flavor, but a fresh appearance as well. The Rosemary Martini is perfect for garden parties, baby showers, or any other occasion where you wish to celebrate both nature and life.

INGREDIENTS:

4 parts Bombay Sapphire gin
1 part dry vermouth
1 sprig rosemary, plus 1 more for garnish

DIRECTIONS:

1. Add gin, vermouth, and the rosemary sprig to a cocktail shaker filled with ice.
2. Shake well.
3. Strain the resulting mixture into a cocktail glass.
4. Garnish with the remaining sprig of rosemary.

STRAWBERRY BASIL MARTINI

Strawberry and basil go well together, so it makes sense that they work well together in a sweet martini. By using sweet vermouth and muddling a bit of fresh strawberry and basil, you can create an enticing medley of flavors that you never expected to taste within a martini. The Strawberry Basil Martini is fresh, fruity, and herbal, making it a refreshing addition to any mixologist's repertoire.

INGREDIENTS:

4 parts gin
1 part sweet vermouth
2 fresh strawberries, plus 1 slice for garnish
2 basil leaves, plus 1 for garnish

DIRECTIONS:

1. At the bottom of a cocktail shaker, muddle 2 strawberries and 2 basil leaves with the sweet vermouth.
2. Add ice and gin to the shaker.
3. Shake well.
4. Strain the resulting mixture into a cocktail glass.
5. Garnish with a slice of strawberry and float a basil leaf atop the drink.

CRANTINI

Similar to the famous Cosmopolitan cocktail, the Crantini is made with cranberry liqueur rather than fresh cranberry juice. The resulting cocktail has a little less sweetness and a little more bite than its pink cousin, providing the Cosmo-averse with a way to enjoy the flavor of cranberry without sugar overwhelming their palate.

INGREDIENTS:

3 parts gin
1 part triple sec
1 part cranberry liqueur
1 lime wheel, for garnish

DIRECTIONS:

1. Add gin, triple sec, and cranberry liqueur to a mixing glass filled with ice.
2. Stir thoroughly.
3. Strain the resulting mixture into a cocktail glass.
4. Garnish with a lime wheel.

WHITE WINE MARTINI

It's surprising that the White Wine Martini isn't a more common cocktail, since one of the primary ingredients in the martini—vermouth—is a fortified herbal wine. The White Wine Martini strips down this particular ingredient to its simplest elements, providing a sweet counterpoint to the gin without sacrificing the clarity and elegance of the cocktail. Outside of traditional drinks like sangria, wine cocktails are rare, so white wine enthusiasts will surely want to try this one.

INGREDIENTS:

2 parts gin
1 part white wine
3 grapes, for garnish

DIRECTIONS:

1. Add gin and white wine to a mixing glass filled with ice.
2. Stir thoroughly.
3. Strain the resulting mixture into a cocktail glass.
4. Garnish with three grapes on a toothpick.

MARTINI SHOOTER

The Martini Shooter isn't so much a flavor variant as it is a miniaturized version of the cocktail. It's fun and whimsical—after all, who would ever think to turn the fabled martini into a shot? The Martini Shooter is a great way to celebrate the spirit of this famous cocktail without feeling like you ought to be wearing a tuxedo while drinking it.

INGREDIENTS:

1 oz. gin
¼ oz. dry vermouth
1 dash olive brine
1 pimento-stuffed olive, for garnish

DIRECTIONS:

1. Add the gin, vermouth, and olive brine to a cocktail shaker filled with ice.
2. Shake well.
3. Strain the resulting mixture into a shot glass.
4. Drop a pimento-stuffed olive to the bottom of the glass for garnish.

7

VODKA MARTINIS
AND VARIATIONS

"Call me what you like, only give me some vodka."

RUSSIAN PROVERB

VODKA MARTINIS

The classic version of a martini is made with gin—there can be no argument there. But there can also be no argument that the vodka martini has accrued a following of its own, with many settling into the familiar, comforting arms of that most popular of liquors.

While gin purists may turn their noses up at this claim, the truth is that the vodka martini is no less elegant, no less flavorful, and, frankly, no less perfect than the gin iteration. It simply makes use of a different primary ingredient, one that possesses different strengths and weaknesses—particularly when it comes to its flavored variants.

You'll notice that the standard recipes in this chapter don't deviate much from their gin counterparts. This is by design. Gin lovers are not alone in their appreciation of the beautiful simplicity of the martini cocktail. Vodka devotees are similarly reverent of the original martini recipe, and just as eager to maintain the delicate balance of flavors that have helped the drink stand the test of time.

Even the most ardent of gin lovers would do well to sample the options presented here. View it as a great opportunity to expand your horizons. You may find that you prefer to remain loyal to the gin-centric classic, which is perfectly fine. Or you may find an entirely new reason to love the martini.

CLASSIC VODKA MARTINI

One of the beautiful things about the martini is that, whether you prefer it with gin or vodka, there is no need to overthink it. Simply add vermouth in the ratio you prefer and you're blessed with a delicious cocktail. The use of Skyy vodka gives the Classic Vodka Martini a simple, elegant feeling. Like the cocktail itself, Skyy isn't overcomplicated. It offers a classic vodka experience—making it perfect for inclusion in this most famous of cocktails.

INGREDIENTS:

4 parts Skyy vodka
1 part dry vermouth
1 lemon twist, for garnish

DIRECTIONS:

1. Add the vodka and vermouth to a mixing glass filled with ice.
2. Stir until thoroughly mixed.
3. Strain the resulting mixture into a cocktail glass.
4. Garnish with a twist of lemon.

HIGHBROW VODKA MARTINI

Grey Goose calls itself "the world's best-tasting vodka," and even those who struggle to drink vodka without thoroughly mixing it will agree that Grey Goose is incredibly smooth. This renowned drinkability makes Grey Goose a popular choice among martini enthusiasts who are looking to elevate their cocktail to the next level. The addition of the vermouth perfectly accents the round flavor of the vodka, giving any martini made with Grey Goose a decidedly fancy feel.

INGREDIENTS:

4 parts Grey Goose vodka
1 part dry vermouth
1 lemon twist, for garnish

DIRECTIONS:

1. Add the vodka and vermouth to a mixing glass filled with ice.
2. Stir until thoroughly mixed.
3. Strain the resulting mixture into a cocktail glass.
4. Garnish with a twist of lemon.

BUDGET VODKA MARTINI

Like the gin version, the vodka martini is a classic anyone can enjoy—even those on a budget. While more expensive vodkas may be more popular in cocktails, the truth is that there are plenty of delicious and affordable options available. Those on a tighter budget should consider Svedka vodka, an option that retains the drinkability of its more expensive brethren.

INGREDIENTS:

4 parts Svedka vodka
1 part dry vermouth
1 dash lemon juice

DIRECTIONS:

1. Add the vodka, vermouth, and lemon juice to a mixing glass filled with ice.
2. Stir until thoroughly mixed.
3. Strain the resulting mixture into a cocktail glass.

DRY VODKA MARTINI

Fans of gin aren't the only ones who turn to a martini to get their fix. Vodka lovers, too, occasionally prefer a more generous vodka-to-vermouth ratio to get their fill of their favorite spirit. For those individuals, there is the Dry Vodka Martini. It's not a drink for the faint of heart, and those who wish to sample it should make sure they use high-quality vodka. But individuals with the proper appreciation for vodka will be hard-pressed to find a purer cocktail.

INGREDIENTS:

8 parts vodka
1 part dry vermouth
1 lemon twist, for garnish

DIRECTIONS:

1. Add the vodka and vermouth to a mixing glass filled with ice.
2. Stir until thoroughly mixed.
3. Strain the resulting mixture into a cocktail glass.
4. Garnish with a twist of lemon.

WET VODKA MARTINI

If there's a dry martini, surely there must be a wet version, right? Since "dry" signifies more gin or vodka, "wet" generally signifies less. Those who enjoy their martini on the wet side generally love the flavor of vermouth, and wet martinis approaching a 1:1 ratio of vodka to vermouth are not uncommon. This recipe doesn't go quite that far, but it will certainly challenge your beliefs about vermouth.

INGREDIENTS:

2 parts vodka
1 part dry vermouth
1 lime twist, for garnish

DIRECTIONS:

1. Add vodka and vermouth to a mixing glass filled with ice.
2. Stir until thoroughly mixed.
3. Strain the resulting mixture into a cocktail glass.
4. Garnish with a twist of lime.

PERFECT VODKA MARTINI

The Perfect Vodka Martini isn't as widespread as the Perfect Martini, but a half-sweet vermouth, half-dry vermouth vodka martini sounds no less delicious than the gin version. The Perfect Vodka Martini calls for a bit less vodka than its gin counterpart in order to give the sweet vermouth a chance to shine, but still packs a significant punch—all without skimping on flavor.

INGREDIENTS:

4 parts vodka
1 part dry vermouth
1 part sweet vermouth
1 lemon twist, for garnish

DIRECTIONS:

1. Add the vodka and vermouths to a mixing glass filled with ice.
2. Stir until thoroughly mixed.
3. Strain the resulting mixture into a cocktail glass.
4. Garnish with a twist of lemon.

SWEET VODKA MARTINI

Moving one step past the Perfect Vodka Martini is the Sweet Vodka Martini. This one calls for a bit less vodka than the standard vodka martini, with the intention of letting the sweet elements stand out. Fans of vodka drinks on the sweet side will surely love this variant!

INGREDIENTS:

3 parts vodka
1 part sweet vermouth
1 maraschino cherry, for garnish

DIRECTIONS:

1. Add the vodka and vermouth to a mixing glass filled with ice.
2. Stir until thoroughly mixed.
3. Strain the resulting mixture into a cocktail glass.
4. Garnish with a maraschino cherry on a toothpick.

DIRTY VODKA MARTINI

The saltiness of olive brine complements gin and vodka equally well, and vodka drinkers who have never had occasion to try a classic Dirty Martini would be wise to give this drink a try. Olive brine may not sound like the most appetizing of ingredients, but, as with many cocktails, even the strangest ingredients can add a delicious element when properly employed.

INGREDIENTS:

4 parts vodka
1 part dry vermouth
1 splash olive brine
3 pimento-stuffed olives, for garnish

DIRECTIONS:

1. Add the vodka, vermouth, and olive brine to a mixing glass filled with ice.
2. Stir until thoroughly mixed.
3. Strain the resulting mixture into a cocktail glass.
4. Garnish with pimento-stuffed olives on a toothpick.

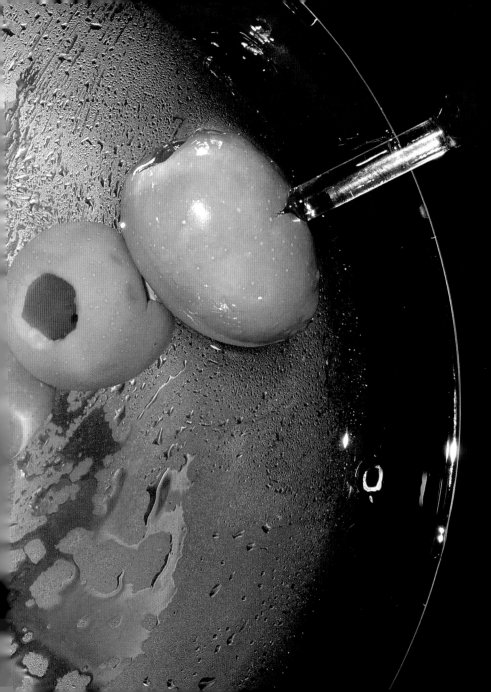

FILTHY VODKA MARTINI

Those who find themselves liking the Dirty Vodka Martini should go one step further and sample the Filthy Vodka Martini. Like its gin-based counterpart, the Filthy Vodka Martini adds blue cheese to the mix, providing a tangy element to the traditionally smooth cocktail. It may sound strange, but if you're hesitant, just ask yourself: When has adding cheese to something ever been a bad idea?

INGREDIENTS:

4 parts vodka
1 part dry vermouth
1 splash olive brine
3 blue cheese-stuffed olives, for garnish
1 handful blue cheese crumbles, for garnish

DIRECTIONS:

1. Add the vodka, vermouth, and olive brine to a mixing glass filled with ice.
2. Stir until thoroughly mixed.
3. Strain the resulting mixture into a cocktail glass.
4. Crumble a small amount of blue cheese over the drink.
5. Garnish with blue cheese-stuffed olives on a toothpick.

VODKA MARTINI SHOOTER

As with gin, we close the martini section with a shooter. The Vodka Martini Shooter might be even more inviting than the gin version, as vodka is a liquor that lends itself slightly better to shots. A little splash of vermouth and a tiny hint of olive brine make this shooter a perfect little mouthful of vodka martini.

INGREDIENTS:

1 oz. vodka
¼ oz. dry vermouth
1 dash olive brine
1 pimento-stuffed olive, for garnish

DIRECTIONS:

1. Add the vodka, vermouth, and olive brine to a cocktail shaker filled with ice.
2. Shake well.
3. Strain the resulting mixture into a shot glass.
4. Garnish by balancing an olive on a toothpick over the center of the shot glass.

"I began to think vodka was my drink at last. It didn't taste like anything, but it went straight down into my stomach like a sword swallowers' sword and made me feel powerful and godlike."

SYLVIA PLATH, *THE BELL JAR*

VARIATIONS ON VODKA MARTINIS

Even those who are not lovers of vodka will admit that it is the ideal liquor for a number of mixed drinks. This is because, perhaps more than any other type of alcohol, vodka takes on the flavor of anything it is mixed with. It adds bite to apple brandy. It grounds the sourness of lemon. It hides beneath the spice of a jalapeño, waiting to pounce.

This quality makes vodka the perfect choice for many flavored martini variants. Unlike gin, vodka imparts little flavor on its own. By not forcing the other ingredients to stand up to a bold flavor like juniper, vodka greatly expands your options when it comes to fun and whimsical takes on the martini.

Fans of the classic Appletini need only turn the page and whip one up for themselves. Raspberry fans, espresso drinkers, and even those lovers of all things pickled will also find something to tantalize their taste buds here.

Whether or not you consider a vodka martini a "true" martini, it's impossible to deny the incredible versatility of this delicious spirit and the martini riffs it inspire.

APPLETINI

Perhaps the most popular martini variant, the Appletini combines the bite of the vodka with the sour pucker of apple to create a drink that is both flavorful and visually striking. Traditionally made with a green apple liqueur to give the drink a vibrant hue, the Appletini is a little bit sweet, a little bit sour, and extremely beautiful.

INGREDIENTS:

3 parts vodka
1 part Sour Apple Pucker
1 part triple sec
3 apple slices, for garnish

DIRECTIONS:

1. Add the vodka, Sour Apple Pucker, and triple sec to a cocktail shaker filled with ice.
2. Shake well.
3. Strain the resulting mixture into a cocktail glass.
4. Garnish with three thin apple slices on a skewer.

The Appletini is one of many martini variations that eliminates the vermouth in favor of other, more flavorful ingredients. That said, many of these cocktails can be slightly altered by adding the vermouth back in, giving the drink a slightly "dryer" taste and grounding a cocktail you may feel has gotten too sweet.

PINEAPPLE MARTINI

Flavored vodka is great. It opens up a whole new world of potential combinations without forcing you to work with complicated and messy ingredients. That said, the inclusion of fresh fruit is essential to offset the occasional artificial quality of flavored vodka, and you'll find that muddling a bit of fresh pineapple goes a long way in this drink.

INGREDIENTS:

1 part vodka
1 part pineapple vodka
1 splash simple syrup
4 pineapple slices, rind removed; plus 1 more, rind on, for garnish

DIRECTIONS:

1. At the bottom of a cocktail shaker, muddle the 4 pineapple slices and the simple syrup.
2. Add ice, both vodkas, and simple syrup to the shaker.
3. Shake well.
4. Strain the resulting mixture into a cocktail glass.
5. Garnish with a pineapple slice.

LYCHEETINI

The lychee isn't an ingredient most people are familiar with, which is a shame. It's a sweet, fleshy, bite-sized fruit that makes for the perfect garnish—and the perfect addition to a drink. The flavor of the lychee is both sweet and delicate, and the elegant look of the fruit makes it ideal for inclusion in a martini. The Lycheetini is an excellent wedding cocktail.

INGREDIENTS:

3 parts vodka
1 part triple sec
2 parts lychee liqueur
1 lychee, for garnish

DIRECTIONS:

1. Add the vodka, triple sec, and lychee liqueur to a cocktail shaker filled with ice.
2. Shake well.
3. Strain the resulting mixture into a cocktail glass.
4. Garnish with a lychee on a toothpick.

Lychee liqueur can be hard to find, but there are alternatives. You can usually find lychees in a jar, and you can use some of the liquid from the jar in place of the liqueur, adding a bit more vodka to make up for it. When you find yourself in a jam like this, just get creative!

SOUR CHERRY MARTINI

Adding a bit of sour to the martini is not a new concept (see the Lemon Drop cocktail on page 133), but few recipes have done it better than the Sour Cherry Martini. Cherry and lime go together about as well as peanut butter and jelly, and the Sour Cherry Martini pits the sweet and sour elements of those two fruits against the welcome bite of the vodka to create a cocktail that celebrates the beauty of each ingredient.

INGREDIENTS:

1 part vodka
2 parts cherry vodka
1 part lime juice
1 dash grenadine
1 lime wheel, for garnish
1 maraschino cherry, for garnish

DIRECTIONS:

1. Add vodka, cherry vodka, grenadine, and lime juice to a cocktail shaker filled with ice.
2. Shake vigorously.
3. Strain resulting mixture into a cocktail glass.
4. Garnish with a lime wheel and a maraschino cherry.

BELLINI MARTINI

The Bellini is a beloved peach-and-champagne cocktail, but it also rhymes with martini. Coincidence? Almost certainly. Still, the Bellini Martini incorporates the best elements of both drinks, resulting in a sweet, fizzy, and flavorful treat sure to delight the palate.

INGREDIENTS:

2 parts vodka
1 part peach schnapps
1 part champagne
1 splash simple syrup
1 peach slice, for garnish

DIRECTIONS:

1. Add vodka, peach schnapps, and simple syrup to a cocktail shaker filled with ice.
2. Shake vigorously.
3. Add champagne to the cocktail shaker.
4. Stir gently.
5. Strain the resulting mixture into a cocktail glass.
6. Garnish with a slice of peach.

Garnishes generally aren't intended to be eaten, but you can always change things up. For instance, with the Espresso Martini, why not add chocolate-covered coffee beans instead of regular coffee beans and give yourself a delicious treat when you're done sipping?

ESPRESSO MARTINI

While the Breakfast Martini incorporates many of the popular breakfast flavors into one cohesive cocktail, the Espresso Martini is only interested in one flavor: coffee. The perfect wake-up cocktail, it includes espresso, coffee liqueur, and vodka, a mixture of ingredients that all contain their fair share of kick. After shaking them together, you should find a light froth at the top of the cocktail, upon which you can rest a few coffee beans.

INGREDIENTS:

3 parts vodka
1 part Kahlua, or other coffee liqueur
2 parts espresso
1 handful coffee beans, for garnish

DIRECTIONS:

1. Add vodka, Kahlua, and espresso to a cocktail shaker filled with ice.
2. Shake well.
3. Strain the resulting mixture into a cocktail glass.
4. Garnish with coffee beans.

RASPBERRY MARTINI

Raspberry is an obvious flavor to incorporate into a vodka martini. While the sour nature of the fruit might struggle to stand up to the juniper present in gin, it is a perfect partner for vodka—and does a particularly good job bringing out the flavor already present in raspberry vodka. The Raspberry Martini is a little bit sweet and a little bit sour, uniting several different flavor elements into a whole that might just be more than the sum of its parts.

INGREDIENTS:

2 parts vodka
1 part raspberry vodka
1 part triple sec
1 splash simple syrup
5 raspberries, plus 3 more for garnish

DIRECTIONS:

1. At the bottom of a cocktail shaker, muddle 5 raspberries with the simple syrup.
2. Add ice, both vodkas, and triple sec to the shaker.
3. Shake well.
4. Strain the resulting mixture into a cocktail glass.
5. Garnish by floating 3 raspberries atop the cocktail.

STRAWBERRY KIWITINI

Strawberry and kiwi are a beloved combination, and here they add a fresh, tropical element to the martini. The use of fresh strawberries and kiwis is a must—strawberry liqueur often has a medicinal quality to it that simply won't do in a cocktail where the balance between flavors is as delicate as it is in the martini. The Strawberry Kiwitini is lightly rosy, beautifully crisp, and goes down incredibly easy.

INGREDIENTS:

6 parts vodka
1 part dry vermouth
1 splash simple syrup
2 strawberries, plus 1 slice for garnish
3 kiwi slices, peeled

DIRECTIONS:

1. At the bottom of a cocktail shaker, muddle the strawberries and 3 kiwi slices with the simple syrup.
2. Add ice, vodka, and vermouth to the shaker.
3. Shake well.
4. Strain the resulting mixture into a cocktail glass.
5. Garnish with a sliced strawberry.

PICKLED MARTINI

If adding olive brine makes a martini "dirty," what does adding pickle juice make it? Pickled, of course. The Pickled Martini is a simple take on the Dirty Martini, swapping pickle juice for olive brine and using a cornichon for garnish. It's an interesting alternative to an already popular recipe, and one that pickle lovers are sure to enjoy.

INGREDIENTS:

4 parts vodka
1 part dry vermouth
1 splash pickle juice
1 cornichon, for garnish

DIRECTIONS:

1. Add the vodka, vermouth, and pickle juice to a mixing glass filled with ice.
2. Stir until thoroughly mixed.
3. Strain the resulting mixture into a cocktail glass.
4. Garnish with one or more cornichons on a toothpick.

SPICY MARTINI

Pepper-stuffed olives are a popular cocktail garnish, even for cocktails not intended to incorporate spice. So why not amp up the spiciness of the pepper and then add a little heat to the cocktail itself? The Spicy Martini incorporates jalapeño into the cocktail itself, and invites those who want a little bit more to chomp down on the spicy garnish accompanying the drink.

INGREDIENTS:

4 parts vodka
1 part dry vermouth
1 dash jalapeño hot sauce
2 jalapeño-stuffed olives, for garnish

DIRECTIONS:

1. Add vodka, vermouth, and hot sauce to a cocktail shaker filled with ice.
2. Shake vigorously.
3. Strain resulting mixture into a cocktail glass.
4. Garnish with the jalapeño-stuffed olives on a toothpick.

✦ 8 ✦

IN THE SPIRIT: SIMILARLY SIMPLE SOLUTIONS

> "The beauty of the cosmos derives not only of unity in variety, but also from variety in unity."
>
> UMBERTO ECO, *THE NAME OF THE ROSE*

IN THE SPIRIT: SIMILARLY SIMPLE SOLUTIONS

While the martini is celebrated in large part for its simplicity, it is far from the only cocktail to feature a refined minimalism and outstanding taste. In fact, plenty of other cocktails share the martini's sense of austere dignity, and they come in many shapes, sizes, and colors.

Whiskey lovers will rightly put forth the Manhattan as a counterpoint to the martini. Citrus lovers will tout the Gimlet. Cognac fans will point to the Sidecar, or even the Sazerac. The point is, if you enjoy a good martini and are looking to branch out, there are plenty of options available.

What follows is a selection of cocktails that span many different alcohol types, flavor profiles, serving vessels, and appearances. They run the gamut from sweet to savory, and clear to cloudy, but they all have something in common with the martini—a simplicity that has carried them into the pantheon of cocktails.

THE MARTINEZ

The Martinez is mentioned in the "History of the Martini" section as the rumored basis of the cocktail, so it was the obvious choice to be the lead recipe here. While it's impossible to verify the connection this drink has to today's martini, it remains a delicious drink that bears a striking resemblance to the popular cocktail. The Martinez is on the sweeter side, but incorporates ingredients that are not unfamiliar to those who have sampled a wide range of martini variants.

INGREDIENTS:

3 parts gin
1 part sweet vermouth
1 part maraschino liqueur
1 dash bitters
1 maraschino cherry, for garnish
1 lemon slice, for garnish

DIRECTIONS:

1. Add the gin, vermouth, maraschino liqueur, and bitters to a mixing glass filled with ice.
2. Stir thoroughly.
3. Strain the resulting mixture into a cocktail glass.
4. Garnish with a maraschino cherry and lemon slice.

If you don't have maraschino liqueur—an admittedly uncommon ingredient—you can always improvise and use some of the liquid from a jar of maraschino cherries instead. You may want to use a light hand, though—it's very sweet and very concentrated.

LEMON DROP

The Lemon Drop is a popular cocktail, combining a little sweetness with a taste of sour. A take on the vodka martini, the Lemon Drop adds a bit of orange, a bit of lemon, and a dusting of sugar. Considerably sweeter than most traditional cocktails, the Lemon Drop is the perfect alternative for those who find the bite of a classic vodka martini to be a bit much.

INGREDIENTS:

2 parts vodka
1 part triple sec
1 part lemon juice
Sugar, for the rim
1 lemon twist, for garnish

DIRECTIONS:

1. Combine vodka, triple sec, and lemon juice in a cocktail shaker filled with ice.
2. Shake well.
3. Wet the rim of a cocktail glass and then dip it into the sugar.
4. Strain the cocktail shaker into the cocktail glass.
5. Garnish with a twist of lemon.

NEGRONI

Where the Lemon Drop combines sweet and sour, the Negroni mixes sweet and savory to perfection. The slight bitterness from both the gin and the bitters counter the Campari and sweet vermouth perfectly, and the equal portions of each ingredient make for a perfectly balanced cocktail. Although mixologists debate whether the true recipe should include bitters, you'll find that their addition adds a little something extra to an already delicious drink.

INGREDIENTS:

1 part gin
1 part Campari
1 part sweet vermouth
1 dash bitters
1 orange slice, for garnish

DIRECTIONS:

1. Fill a mixing glass with ice and add the gin, Campari, sweet vermouth, and bitters.
2. Stir until thoroughly mixed.
3. Strain the resulting mixture into an Old Fashioned glass filled with ice.
4. Garnish with an orange slice.

"The bitters are excellent for your liver, the gin is bad for you. They balance each other."

ORSON WELLES,
on the Negroni

MANHATTAN

Simple, elegant, and delicious, the Manhattan is whiskey's answer to the martini. Whiskey drinkers will no doubt be familiar with the cocktail already, but fans of the martini who are looking to branch out may wish to experiment with this flavorful cocktail. Replace the gin with rye whiskey, swap out dry vermouth for sweet vermouth, add a dash of bitters—and presto! You've transformed your martini into a Manhattan.

INGREDIENTS:

3 parts rye whiskey
1 part sweet vermouth
1 dash bitters
1 maraschino cherry, for garnish

DIRECTIONS:

1. Add the whiskey, sweet vermouth, and bitters to a mixing glass filled with ice.
2. Stir until thoroughly mixed.
3. Strain the resulting mixture into a cocktail glass with the desired amount of ice.
4. Garnish with a maraschino cherry.

COSMOPOLITAN

The Cosmopolitan is another sweet take on the vodka martini, this time adding cranberry and lime to the mix. Famous for its pink hue, the Cosmopolitan (or "Cosmo," as it is colloquially known) combines a few simple ingredients into a delicious cocktail that balances a surprising range of flavors. The slight bitterness of the cranberry, the sourness of the lime, and the sweetness of the triple sec all come together beautifully, standing up well to the bite of the vodka.

INGREDIENTS:

2 parts vodka
1 part triple sec
1 part cranberry juice
1 splash lime juice
1 lime wheel, for garnish

DIRECTIONS:

1. Add vodka, triple sec, cranberry juice, and lime juice to a cocktail shaker filled with ice.
2. Shake well.
3. Strain the resulting mixture into a cocktail glass.
4. Garnish with a lime wheel.

GIMLET

Similar to the Lime Martini, the Gimlet is a classic cocktail that eliminates the vermouth entirely in favor of a purer experience of the lime. Where a classic martini favors the subtle flavor of vermouth, the Gimlet goes all in on sour, resulting in a cocktail that retains the grace and dignity of the martini, but presents a sharper, less stately facade.

INGREDIENTS:

4 parts gin
1 part fresh lime juice
1 lime wheel, for garnish

DIRECTIONS:

1. Add the gin and lime juice to a cocktail shaker filled with ice.
2. Shake vigorously.
3. Strain the resulting mixture into a cocktail glass.
4. Garnish with a lime wheel.

TEQUILA MARTINI

Why let gin and vodka have all the fun? It's a question that tequila drinkers have asked for ages. The truth is, there's no reason not to mix a martini using tequila, rum, or any other liquor you prefer ... as long as you're prepared to provide proper balance. In fact, the Tequila Martini is similar to the Margarita, substituting vermouth for the usual triple sec, and adjusting the ratios to compensate.

INGREDIENTS:

4 parts silver tequila
1 part dry vermouth
1 part fresh lime juice
Salt, for the rim
1 lime wheel, for garnish

DIRECTIONS:

1. Add the tequila, vermouth, and lime juice to a cocktail shaker filled with ice.
2. Shake vigorously.
3. Wet the rim of a cocktail glass and then dip it into the salt.
4. Strain the contents of the cocktail shaker into the cocktail glass.
5. Garnish with a lime wheel.

SIDECAR

The Sidecar is a martini variation primarily due to presentation, as its beautiful simplicity mirrors that of the famous gin cocktail. In many ways, the Sidecar is cognac's answer to the martini, with just two other ingredients to stand up against cognac's powerful flavor. The orange-brown hue of this simple cocktail radiates sunlight, brightening your day with every sip.

INGREDIENTS:

3 parts cognac
1 part triple sec
1 part lemon juice
1 orange wedge, for garnish

DIRECTIONS:

1. Add cognac, triple sec, and lemon juice to a cocktail shaker filled with ice.
2. Shake vigorously.
3. Strain the resulting mixture into a cocktail glass.
4. Garnish with an orange wedge.

SAZERAC

The Sazerac is another popular cognac-based cocktail, this time incorporating the unusual flavor of absinthe. Absinthe is a strong liqueur; its effects upon the drinker are somewhat shrouded in mystery and legend—a fact that has no doubt contributed to the popularity of the Sazerac. This is a slightly more complicated cocktail to construct, requiring two separate glasses for preparation, and making use of the "rinse" technique that is used to coat the inside of a glass. It may seem like a lot, but the Sazerac is a cocktail well worth the effort.

INGREDIENTS:

4 parts cognac
1 part absinthe
1 sugar cube
2 dashes bitters
1 lemon twist, for garnish

DIRECTIONS:

1. Use the absinthe to lightly rinse the inside of an Old Fashioned glass, then add ice.
2. In a separate mixing glass, muddle the sugar cube with the bitters.
3. Add the cognac to the glass containing the sugar and bitters, along with ice.
4. Stir the cognac, sugar, and bitters thoroughly.
5. Discard the ice from absinthe-coated glass.
6. Strain the cognac, sugar, and bitters mixture into the absinthe-coated glass.
7. Garnish with a twist of lemon.

FRENCH 75

We close with the celebratory cocktail known as the French 75. Traditionally served in a champagne flute, the French 75 combines gin and champagne for a drink that is a little fizzy, a little lemony, and more than a little dignified. The cocktail is popular at weddings and celebrations, as its beautiful golden color gives it an opulent feel. The French 75 can be prepared sweet or dry, depending on your taste in champagne.

INGREDIENTS:

1 part gin
2 parts champagne
Juice from 1 lemon wedge
1 dash simple syrup
1 lemon twist, for garnish

DIRECTIONS:

1. Add the gin, simple syrup, and lemon juice to a cocktail shaker filled with ice.
2. Shake vigorously.
3. Strain the resulting mixture into a champagne flute.
4. Top with champagne.
5. Gently stir the ingredients together, if desired.
6. Garnish with the lemon twist.

9

GIN DISTILLERS AND VERMOUTH PRODUCERS

LOVE IS LIKE A BOTTLE OF GIN

But A Bottle Of Gin Is Not Like Love

GIN DISTILLERS

With so many martini recipes to choose from, where to start? When mixing a martini, the gin you choose can greatly impact the drink's flavor. Whether you select a popular top-shelf brand such as Bombay Sapphire or Plymouth, or reach for a more affordable brand such as New Amsterdam, you'll notice subtle differences in flavor that go beyond the simple "top shelf" and "bottom of the barrel" distinctions.

The botanicals used in a given type of gin are perhaps the greatest differentiator. When learning about different gin brands, there are certain botanicals you'll see pop up time and again: juniper, licorice, lemon, and angelica root, for instance, are popular flavoring agents. But you'll also discover some gins that choose to infuse more uncommon flavors: Hendrick's, for example, is known for infusing rose and cucumber into its spirits.

In this section, you'll find profiles of some of the more popular gin makers, along with recommended products for use in a martini. You'll learn about their countries of origin, the botanicals used to flavor them, and see a brief description from the distillers themselves.

Which gin is best? It's a question that has no answer. Sample a wide variety and you might find that the inclusion of coriander pleases your taste buds. You might find that Hendrick's inclusion of cucumber makes a big difference to you, or you might find that a more affordable gin option tastes just as good as its top-shelf contemporaries. In a cocktail as simple and elegant as the martini, small flavor differences can have a huge ripple effect —so try as many different gins as possible and decide which one is best for you.

TANQUERAY

Brand Name: Tanqueray
Country of Origin: England
Manufacturer: Diageo
Website: tanqueray.com

Recommended for Martinis: Tanqueray London Dry Gin
Introduced: 1830
ABV: 47.3% (U.S.)
Key Botanicals: Angelica Root | Coriander | Juniper Berries | Licorice

How Tanqueray Describes It: "Fortune favours the brave. Back in the 1830's Charles Tanqueray wasn't afraid to mix his bold ideas. His ingenious pursuit for perfection paid off, creating Tanqueray London Dry, a perfectly balanced gin and one of the most awarded gins in the world."

Availability: Tanqueray products, including London Dry Gin, are widely available in the United States and throughout the world.

How to Recognize It: The uniquely shaped, distinctive green bottle has become synonymous with Tanqueray gin.

Other Products: Tanqueray Rangpur, Tanqueray No. TEN

TANQUERAY EXTRA DRY MARTINI

INGREDIENTS:

1¼ oz. Tanqueray London Dry Gin
2 to 4 dashes dry French vermouth
1 small, pitted Spanish cocktail olive, for garnish

DIRECTIONS:

1. Pour vermouth into a mixing glass over ice, roll around, then strain out.
2. Add Tanqueray London Dry Gin and stir.
3. Strain into a cocktail glass.
4. Garnish with a small, pitted Spanish cocktail olive.

BOMBAY SAPPHIRE

Brand Name: Bombay Sapphire
Country of Origin: England
Manufacturer: Bombay Spirits Co., Ltd.
Website: bombaysapphire.com

Introduced: 1987
ABV: 47% (U.S.)
Key Botanicals: Almond | Angelica | Cassia | Coriander | Cubeb Berry | Grains of Paradise | Juniper Berries | Lemon Peel | Licorice | Orris Root

How Bombay Describes It: "Born of our passion for excellence and infused with ten exotic botanicals, Bombay Sapphire has a clean, bright flavor with a vibrant, peppery finish."

Availability: Bombay Sapphire and other Bombay products are widely available in the United States and throughout the world.

How to Recognize It: Bombay Sapphire is available in a unique blue bottle that makes it easy to spot on the shelf.

Other Products from Bombay Spirits: Bombay Sapphire East, Bombay Dry Gin, Star of Bombay

NEW AMSTERDAM

Brand Name: New Amsterdam
Country of Origin: United States
Manufacturer: New Amsterdam Spirits Company
Website: newamsterdamspirits.com

Recommended for Martinis: New Amsterdam Gin
ABV: 40%
Key Botanicals: Unknown

How New Amsterdam Describes It: "New Amsterdam Gin is crafted with botanicals, citrus, and a nod to juniper. As one of the best gins available, it's a modern take on the 400-year tradition. The smooth finish lets you drink this flavorful gin straight or as the centerpiece of a perfect martini."

Availability: New Amsterdam is one of the fastest growing gin (and vodka) brands in the United States. It is readily available throughout the U.S.

How to Recognize It: New Amsterdam products are bottled in recognizably tapered bottles with New Amsterdam printed down the center.

Other Products: New Amsterdam Vodka

BEEFEATER

Brand Name: Beefeater Gin
Country of Origin: England
Manufacturer: James Burrough Ltd.
Website: beefeatergin.com

Recommended for Martinis: Beefeater London Dry Gin
Introduced: 1876
ABV: 47% (U.S.)
Key Botanicals: Almond | Angelica Root | Angelica Seed | Coriander Seed | Juniper | Lemon Peel | Licorice Root | Orris Root | Seville Orange Peel

How Beefeater Describes It: "One distillery, eight stills, nine botanicals, and three expert distillers produce one bold taste. With every drop made right here in London, we're proud to produce a real London Dry Gin."

Availability: Beefeater products are available in many countries throughout the world, including much of the U.S.

How to Recognize It: The name "Beefeater" refers to the Yeoman Warders, the ceremonial guards of the Tower of London who are colloquially known by the name. Beefeater bottles feature an artistic rendition of one such Beefeater, set before a red-tinged depiction of London.

Other Products: Beefeater 24, Beefeater Burrough's Reserve, Beefeater London Garden

PLYMOUTH

Brand Name: Plymouth Gin
Country of Origin: England
Manufacturer: Pernod Ricard
Website: plymouthgin.com

Recommended for Martinis: Plymouth Gin
Introduced: 1793
ABV: 41.2% (U.S.)
Key Botanicals: Angelica Root | Coriander Seed | Green Cardamom | Juniper Berries | Lemon Peel | Orange Peel | Orris Root

How Plymouth Describes It: "From deep earthy notes to wonderfully fresh juniper and a lemony bite, Plymouth Gin Original's great depth of flavor is just one of the reasons it's truly unique."

Availability: Plymouth Gin is available throughout the United States and much of the world.

How to Recognize It: Plymouth Gin is available in a rounded, light green bottle with a picture of the *Mayflower* on its label.

Other Products: Plymouth Gin Navy Strength, Plymouth Sloe Gin

HENDRICK'S

Brand Name: Hendrick's Gin
Country of Origin: Scotland
Manufacturer: William Grant & Sons
Website: us.hendricksgin.com

Introduced: 1999
ABV: 44% (U.S.)
Key Botanicals: Angelica Root | Caraway | Chamomile | Coriander | Cubeb Berry | Elderflower | Juniper | Lemon | Orange Peel | Orris Root | Yarrow
Infusions: Bulgarian Rosa Damascena | Cucumber

How Hendrick's Describes It: "Hendrick's wondrous botanical signature consists of flowers, roots, fruits, and seeds from the world over. They function to complement and set the stage for our delicious duet of infusions: rose petal and cucumber."

Availability: Hendrick's Gin is available throughout the U.S. and much of the world.

How to Recognize It: Hendrick's Gin comes in a round, brown, apothecary-style bottle that is easy to recognize.

Other Products: There are currently no variants of Hendrick's Gin available, but parent company William Grant & Sons produces other alcohol brands such as Glenfiddich, Tullamore D.E.W., and Sailor Jerry.

LEOPOLD BROS. DISTILLERY

Brand Name: Leopold Bros.
Country of Origin: United States
Website: leopoldbros.com

Recommended for Martinis: Leopold's American Small Batch Gin
Introduced: 2001
ABV: 40%
Key Botanicals: Coriander | Juniper | Orris Root | Pummelos | Velancia Oranges

How Leopold Bros. Describes It: "Most gins are made by simultaneously distilling juniper and other botanicals within the same still. However when boiled together, certain botanicals are overworked, resulting in the extraction of tannin-like flavors which dry out the gin, while other flavors are not fully realized. We distill each botanical: juniper, coriander, pummelos, orris root, Valencia oranges, and more, separately to bring out only the purest flavors and aromas to be blended together for a softer and brighter spirit."

Availability: Leopold Bros. products are available in approximately half of the U.S., as well as in Germany, Spain, the U.K., and numerous other countries throughout the world.

How to Recognize It: Leopold's products come in simple, elegant, clear glass bottles, with a colored wrap around the cork and the brand name and batch number written across the front.

Other Products: Leopold's Navy Strength American Gin, Leopold's Summer Gin, Leopold's Silver Tree American Small Batch Vodka

HARDSHORE DISTILLING COMPANY

Brand Name: Hardshore
Country of Origin: United States
Website: hardshoredistilling.com

Recommended for Martinis: Hardshore Original Gin
Introduced: 2016
ABV: 46%
Key Botanicals: Coriander | Italian Juniper | Mint (Fresh) | Orris Root | Rosemary (Fresh)

How Hardshore Describes It: "Our flagship spirit, Hardshore Original Gin, is a surprisingly complex gin despite being made with only five botanicals. It is bright and distinctive with soft citrus notes and curious hints of iris, mint, and rosemary."

Availability: Hardshore Original Gin is available throughout Maine, New Hampshire, and Massachusetts.

How to Recognize It: Hardshore Original Gin comes in a beautiful, blue-gray bottle with a simple white label featuring the distillery's name.

In 2017, Hardshore Distilling was recognized by USA Today *readers as the Best Craft Gin Distillery in America.*

HARDSHORE MARTINI

INGREDIENTS:

4 oz. Hardshore Original Gin
Dolin Vermouth de Chambery Dry
1 lemon twist, for garnish
1 rosemary sprig, for garnish

DIRECTIONS:

1. Pour a small amount of the vermouth into a cocktail glass.
2. Add gin and ice to a cocktail shaker.
3. Shake hard for 20 seconds.
4. Swirl the vermouth around the cocktail glass, then pour it out.
5. Strain the contents of the shaker into the glass.
6. Garnish with a lemon twist and rosemary sprig.

ST. AUGUSTINE DISTILLERY

Brand Name: St. Augustine Distillery
Country of Origin: United States
Website: staugustinedistillery.com

Recommended for Martinis: New World Gin
Introduced: 2014
ABV: 47%
Key Botanicals: Angelica | Coriander | Juniper

How St. Augustine Describes It: "New World Gin is carefully crafted from the finest botanicals. It has just enough juniper to support good structure, and balanced citrus and spice notes such as cassia bark and angelica. Hand-grinding whole, fresh herbs with a vintage burr mill preserves the freshness and vibrancy of the botanicals in this expression of a classic spirit."

Availability: St. Augustine products are available throughout Florida and the surrounding states.

How to Recognize It: New World Gin comes in the same rounded, long-necked bottle as the rest of St. Augustine's offerings. Corked at the top, the bottles feature the distillery's signature aesthetics alongside the St. Augustine name.

Other Products: Barrel-Finished Gin, Florida Cane Vodka, Port Finished Bourbon, Pot Distilled Rum

NEW HOLLAND ARTISAN SPIRITS

Brand Name: New Holland Artisan Spirits
Country of Origin: United States
Website: newhollandbrew.com

Recommended for Martinis: Knickerbocker Gin
Introduced: 2008
ABV: 42.5%
Key Botanicals: Angelica Root | Cardamom | Cinnamon | Clove | Coriander | Fennel | Ginger Root | Juniper Berry | Lemon Zest | Nutmeg | Orange Zest | Orris Root

How New Holland Describes It: "Knickerbocker Gin is a vibrant, aromatic spirit twice distilled and infused with flavors from more than a dozen herbs and spices. Generous amounts of juniper-berries contribute a bright citrus and evergreen body, bursting with flavor before a clean, dry finish."

Availability: New Holland products are currently available throughout Michigan, as well as Colorado, Connecticut, Illinois, Massachusetts, Minnesota, Nebraska, New Jersey, New York, Wisconsin, and Washington, DC.

How to Recognize It: Knickerbocker Gin comes in an instantly recognizable bottle, deep blue in color with an orange-wrapped top. The name "Knickerbocker" is splashed across the front in a stylized scrawl.

Other Products: Knickerbocker Barrel Gin, Blue Haven Gin, Michigan Awesome Vodka, Dutchess Vodka

ST. GEORGE SPIRITS

Brand Name: St. George Spirits
Country of Origin: United States
Website: stgeorgespirits.com

Recommended for Martinis: Botanivore Gin
Introduced: 2011
ABV: 45%
Key Botanicals: Angelica Root | Bay Laurel | Bergamot Peel | Black Peppercorn | Caraway | Cardamom | Cilantro | Cinnamon | Citra Hops | Coriander | Dill Seed | Fennel Seed | Ginger | Juniper Berries | Lemon Peel | Lime Peel | Orris Root | Seville Orange Peele | Star Anise

How St. George Describes It: "Botanivore, our 'botanical eater,' is comprised of 19 different botanicals working in concert. Think of a meadow in bloom—herbaceous, fresh, and elegant."

Availability: St. George Spirits are available throughout California, many other U.S. states, and several other countries (including Australia, Canada, China, Germany, Panama, Singapore, and the United Kingdom).

How to Recognize It: Botanivore Gin is available in St. George's distinctive barrel-shaped bottles, featuring a vibrant blue label over the cork.

Other Products: Terroir Gin, Dry Rye Gin, All Purpose Vodka, California Citrus Vodka, Green Chile Vodka

ST. GEORGE VESPER

INGREDIENTS:

3 oz. St. George Botanivore Gin
1 oz. St. George All Purpose Vodka
½ oz. Lillet Blanc
1 slice of lemon peel, for garnish

DIRECTIONS:

1. Stir all ingredients with ice to chill (or shake a la 007).
2. Strain into a chilled cocktail glass.
3. Garnish with a thin slice of lemon peel.

"A perfect martini should be made by filling a glass with gin, then waving it in the general direction of Italy."

NOËL COWARD

VERMOUTH PRODUCERS

Although vermouth makes up the lesser part of the martini, your vermouth selection can have just as great an impact on the flavor profile of your drink as your gin selection.

The history of vermouth traces back through England, Germany, France, Italy, and even as far as China, and vermouths from around the world can have very different flavor profiles. Although the basic categories of "dry" and "sweet" vermouth give you a fair idea what to expect, different vermouth makers may choose to place particular emphasis on a particular flavor. This leads to certain vermouth brands being more herbal, others being more citrusy, and still others being sweet, bitter, floral, or any of a dozen other descriptors.

In this section, you'll see brief profiles of a handful of popular vermouth brands, along with descriptions from the makers themselves and recommendations for their use in martinis. A martini is only as good as its ingredients, and choosing the right gin and vermouth for your personal taste can make all the difference.

MARTINI & ROSSI

Brand Name: Martini & Rossi
Country of Origin: Italy
Parent Company: Bacardi
Website: martini.com

Recommended for Martinis: Martini & Rossi Extra Dry
Introduced: 1900
ABV: 15%

How Martini Describes It: "Captured in every drop is the essence of the rare woods, herbs and citrus that make up this secret recipe. Introduced on January 1st, 1900, its sharp citrus aromas and hints of raspberry became a pillar of the cocktail that dominated the century, the Dry Martini cocktail."

Availability: Martini & Rossi vermouth is readily available the world over.

How to Recognize It: Martini & Rossi vermouth comes in a distinctive tall, green bottle with the name Martini boldly placed across the front.

Other Products: Martini & Rossi Bianco, Martini & Rossi Rosso, Martini & Rossi Prosecco

NOILLY PRAT

Brand Name: Noilly Prat
Country of Origin: France
Parent Company: Bacardi
Website: noillyprat.com

Recommended for Martinis:
Noilly Prat Original
Dry Vermouth
Introduced: 1855
ABV: 18%

How Noilly Prat Describes It:
"Aged dry white wines blend-
ed with botanicals, including
Roman chamomile and gentian
from France, bitter orange from
Tunisia and nutmeg from Indonesia."

Availability: Noilly Prat vermouth products
are widely available throughout the world.

How to Recognize It: Noilly Prat products are
generally distributed in an hourglass-shaped bottle.
The Original Dry Vermouth bottle is green in color
and features the brand name in bold letters across
the label.

Other Products: Noilly Prat Extra Dry, Noilly Prat
Rouge, Noilly Prat Ambré

> "Hold it by the stem
> so it will ring."
>
> Culinary legend Julia Child
> insisted on using Noilly Prat for
> her preferred "Upside-Down
> Martini": fill a red-wine glass
> with ice; pour both dry and
> sweet vermouth over ice; float a
> little gin on top and garnish with
> a twist of orange or lemon rind.

GALLO

Brand Name: Gallo Vermouth
Country of Origin: United States
Manufacturer: E&J Gallo Winery
Website: gallo.com

Recommended for Martinis: Gallo Dry Vermouth
Introduced: N/A
ABV: 16%

How Gallo Describes It: "A sweet wine nose with a citrus kick leads to a clean refreshing palate that compliments [*sic*] any Dry Martini. Can also be enjoyed chilled or on the rocks as a flavorful digestif."

Availability: Gallo vermouth is available throughout the United States.

How to Recognize It: Gallo Dry Vermouth comes in a green bottle with a green-tinted, old-fashioned label that is reminiscent of an official seal.

Other Products: Gallo Sweet Vermouth

IMBUE

Brand Name: Imbue
Country of Origin: United States
Manufacturer: Imbue Cellars
Website: imbuecellars.com/

Recommended for Martinis: Imbue Classic Dry Vermouth
Introduced: N/A
ABV: 16.5%

How Imbue Describes It: "Imbue Classic Dry Vermouth is our newest creation. While we love challenging ourselves to create new, innovative aperitifs we also wanted to honor the classic vermouths that paved the way. Meet our classic Dry Vermouth: produced from wine that is barrel aged for 2 to 4 years and infused with wormwood and other bewitching botanicals."

Availability: Imbue is produced in Oregon and can be found in stores in some states. Bottles may also be purchased online from Imbue's website.

How to Recognize It: Imbue comes in a tall wine bottle featuring a green leaf that stands behind the Imbue name.

Other Products: Imbue Bittersweet Vermouth, Imbue Petal & Thorn

VYA

Brand Name: Vya
Country of Origin: Madera, California, USA
Manufacturer: Quady Winery
Website: quadywinery.com

Recommended for Martinis: Vya Extra Dry Vermouth
Introduced: 1999
ABV: 17%

How Vya Describes It: "Relax, sip, shut your eyes, and be transported to a mountain meadow on a river of dry white wine, Orange Muscat, angelica, orris, linden, lavender and more…Made in California's San Joaquin Valley from a blend of dry white wine that includes Orange Muscat, Vya Extra Dry is carefully hand infused at Quady Winery with a selection of over fifteen dried herbs. In Vya Extra Dry the flowers and leaves of the plants are used for the infusion and make Vya Extra Dry powerfully herbaceous, crisp, and refreshing. A few of the herbs used include lavender, linden, sage, orris, alfalfa, and angelica. Fresh and aromatic, Vya Extra Dry wakes up the taste buds, and makes a wet martini or an aperitif on the rocks that livens up the end of the day."

Availability: The Vya vermouth line is available at retailers across much of the United States. Products can also be purchased online through the Quady website.

How to Recognize It: The Vya name is instantly recognizable, splashed in large letters across the front of the bottle. The bottle's golden-yellow hue and the label design are both unique and pleasing to the eye.

Other Products: Vya Whisper Dry Vermouth (recommended for vodka martinis), Vya Sweet Vermouth

VYA MARTINI

INGREDIENTS:

1 oz. Vya Extra Dry Vermouth
2 oz. gin (London Dry-style preferred)
1 dash orange bitters
1 lemon twist or olive, for garnish

DIRECTIONS:

1. Combine all ingredients in a shaker or mixing glass.
2. Stir gently until very cold.
3. Strain into chilled glassware.
4. Garnish with lemon twist or olive.

→ 10 ←

WHERE TO ENJOY
A MARTINI

"He knows just how I like my martini: full of alcohol."

HOMER SIMPSON

WHERE TO ENJOY A MARTINI

In the early 1900s, the martini became a cultural phenomenon. This was in no small part due to its popularity among noteworthy figures of the day, including Ernest Hemingway, H. L. Mencken, and others. The drink has become synonymous with class and dignity, to the point that a similar air of refinement pervades the establishments where the cocktail is frequently consumed.

Those interested in both the martini and its cultural significance should check out the bars mentioned in this section. The martini's reputation and influence aren't confined to America, Europe, or even the Western Hemisphere. No, the martini is a cocktail that has traveled the world, and the establishments known to celebrate its unique alchemy know no bounds.

The martini is a cocktail for all to enjoy, and, as they travel the world, fans of the drink should make it a point to visit as many of these legendary watering holes as possible.

DUKES BAR, LONDON

Name: DUKES Bar
Location: DUKES Hotel, London, England
Founded: 1908
Website: dukeshotel.com

Cultural Significance: *The New York Times* once called DUKES "the hotel bar which some say concocts one of the world's best Martinis." Legend has it that Ian Fleming himself first encountered the martini cocktail within the friendly confines of DUKES, a discovery which, if true, has had enormous impact on the cocktail's reputation.

DUKES is located in the St. James's district in the very heart of London, nearly adjacent to Buckingham Palace. The district has long been a cultural hotspot, and DUKES touts the area as the "exclusive retreat of writers, musicians, politicians, and royalty" through the ages. In addition to the famous bar, DUKES Hotel is the perfect place to stay for part of your tour of the martini world.

Why You Should Drink Your Martini Here: Where better to drink a martini than the very place where James Bond's creator first fell in love with the drink? If the connection to fiction's most famous martini lover doesn't sway you, the fact that DUKES is just a stone's throw from Buckingham Palace certainly should. The martini is one of history's most distinguished drinks, and it's hard to think of a place featuring a more aristocratic air than the location of British throne.

'21' CLUB, NEW YORK CITY

Name: '21' Club
Location: New York City, New York, U.S.A.
Founded: 1930
Website: 21club.com

Cultural Significance: The '21' Club became famous as a speakeasy during the Prohibition years, and that notoriety carried over into legitimate (and successful) business once the alcohol ban was lifted. The disappearing bar and secret wine cellar were retired in favor of tasteful decor that has attracted celebrity regulars ranging from Humphrey Bogart in the early 1900s to President Bill Clinton today.

Celebrity regulars have become such a staple of the '21' Club that their website boasts an interactive map noting the favorite tables of their VIPs. It's an impressive list—table 7 alone lists Ernest Hemingway, Henry Kissinger, and Presidents Richard Nixon and George H. W. Bush among its regular occupants.

Why You Should Drink Your Martini Here: Like the martini, '21' Club rose to prominence during Prohibition, and the martini was known to be a favorite cocktail of regulars like Hemingway. Like the martini, the '21' Club is a classic that has not only survived but thrived through the ages, and something feels right about sipping such a dignified cocktail in the very same establishment where the movers and shakers of America enjoyed them for generations.

THE THREE CLUBS, LOS ANGELES

Name: The Three Clubs
Location: Los Angeles, California, U.S.A.
Founded: 1991
Website: threeclubs.com

Cultural Significance: The Three Clubs is something of a throwback, combining the old-world feel of a high-class Hollywood haunt with the simplistic elegance of a classic martini bar. The Three Clubs features all the amenities that its Hollywood clientele has come to expect: leather seats, live music, a smoking patio, and top-notch service.

The bar was founded by Marc Smith and Matthew Webb in the early 1990s, and has evolved considerably over the years. In its early days, it was featured in the movie *Swingers*, but has since become a more intimate setting for those looking to get away from Los Angeles's seedier elements. Rather than a seedy dive, The Three Clubs has become a place to sip an elegant cocktail and rub elbows with the elite.

Why You Should Drink Your Martini Here: The Three Clubs was originally envisioned as a martini bar, and although it has undergone significant changes over the years, it has always remained true to the original vision. It's one of Los Angeles's more famous (and interesting) cocktail bars, with simple, traditional decor that evokes the martini itself.

OLIVER'S LOUNGE, SEATTLE

Name: Oliver's Lounge
Location: Mayflower Park Hotel, Seattle, Washington, U.S.A.
Founded: 1976
Website: mayflowerpark.com

Cultural Significance: Oliver's Lounge was the first "daylight bar" in the entire state of Washington (prior to a change in law, bars were only allowed to be open after sundown). Before Oliver's, the idea of a bar with windows looking out onto the street was positively alien to the citizens of Seattle, and the legacy that went along with that culture shift permeates Oliver's to this very day.

Long famous for its martinis, Oliver's Lounge now hosts the International Martini Classic Challenge, a competition that began as a challenge to local bartenders and has since grown into a wider celebration of the martini. It should come as no surprise that the bar's own Oliver's Classic Martini has won the competition more than half a dozen times.

Why You Should Drink Your Martini Here: Not only does Oliver's carry the torch for cocktail culture in the city of Seattle, it specifically caters to a martini-loving clientele. The International Martini Classic Challenge represents the high esteem in which the bar's patrons and owners hold the classic cocktail, and Oliver's Lounge stands as one of the best places to enjoy a martini in the entire Pacific Northwest.

BAR HEMINGWAY, PARIS

Name: Bar Hemingway
Location: Ritz Hotel, Paris, France
Founded: Disputed
Website: ritzparis.com

Cultural Significance: Ernest Hemingway features prominently in the history of more than one cocktail, but his name appears frequently throughout the history of the martini. Bar Hemingway, unsurprisingly, is named for the famous writer and drinker, and it is said that during his time in Paris, Hemingway spent more time at this bar than any other place. Hemingway was not the only American expatriate to make the bar his home away from home: Cole Porter, Gary Cooper, F. Scott Fitzgerald, and others were known to while away the hours at the famous establishment.

Although the tale is likely embellished, Hemingway was said to have personally "liberated" the Ritz Hotel from German occupation during his time as a war correspondent in World War II. According to legend, Hemingway commandeered a group of soldiers, and, determined to be the first to set foot inside the liberated Ritz, raced to clear it of Germans. Perhaps fortunately for Hemingway, he arrived to find the Germans long departed, and, denied his desired battle, settled in to drink a series of Dry Martinis.

Why You Should Drink Your Martini Here: If Hemingway's fervor for both the Ritz Hotel and its Dry Martinis doesn't fill you with a fever to visit the bar and try one for yourself, it's likely that nothing will. Bar Hemingway has received more than one makeover over the years, but it remains well known for its martinis, and makes a worthwhile stop for any individual interested in the cultural cache of the cocktail.

EARL GREY CAVIAR MARTINI

INGREDIENTS:

45 ml Ketel One Citroen
10 ml Cointreau
15 ml elderflower cordial
5 ml fresh lemon juice
5 ml fresh lime juice
20 ml clear red apple juice
1 piece cucumber

DIRECTIONS:

Muddle, shake and strain into a cocktail glass.
Top up with Earl Grey Tea Caviar
and Earl Grey Tea Foam.

QUINARY, HONG KONG

Name: Quinary
Location: Hong Kong, China
Founded: 2012
Website: quinary.hk

Cultural significance: Renowned bartender Antonio Lai treats his long bar in the Hong Kong's SoHo neighborhood more like a laboratory —Quinary cocktails are crafted using in-house gadgets like a rotary evaporator, and are acclaimed thanks to redistilling and slow-cooking flavored spirts. In this refined space the drinks are truly the stars of the show. Consistently included on lists of the world's best bars, the Quinary menu features reinventions of classic drinks made memorable thanks to unexpected combinations of flavors and aromas.

Why You Should Drink Your Martini Here: The Earl Grey Caviar Martini is the signature drink at Quinary. But it's not what you think: the "caviar" in question here are beads comprised of Earl Grey tea and sodium alginate, which pop in your mouth once they've passed through tea-infused foam, providing a wonderful contrast to the drink's bright, citrusy flavors. This is the drink that put Lai on the map and paved the way for his cocktail empire.

ORIGIN, HONG KONG

Name: Origin
Location: Hong Kong, China
Founded: 2013
Website: originbar.hk

Cultural Significance: Another stellar offering from Antonio Lai, Origin is Hong Kong's first gin-focused bar. While the ingredients of the martini originated in Europe and the drink rose to prominence in the United States, there are plenty of people and establishments in Asia that respect the cocktail. Origin has placed the martini and other gin-centric cocktails at the heart of their business, a move that has, unsurprisingly, met with great success.

Origin features globally recognized mixologists and boasts 15 unique gin infusions. The gin enthusiasts behind the bar have no shortage of modern tools at their disposal, and their infusion methods include "the use of a rotary evaporator for redistilling unique flavors into the gin, and a water-bath and vacuum to slow-cook." Origin is dedicated to bringing a unique gin and martini experience to the Hong Kong marketplace.

Why You Should Drink Your Martini Here: If you find yourself in Hong Kong, you won't find an establishment more dedicated to extracting the right flavors from gin. Origin offers gins from dozens of distillers to go with a carefully crafted menu featuring both classics and timely innovations. In contrast to some of the other establishments on this list, Origin is a refreshing take on the classic gin bar, and one you would do well to visit.

HARRY'S NEW YORK BAR, PARIS

Name: Harry's New York Bar
Location: Paris, France
Founded: 1911
Website: harrysbar.fr

Cultural Significance: Harry's New York Bar is the second bar on this list located in Paris, France, but when you consider that the martini gained significant popularity among American expatriates in Europe during Prohibition, it begins to make sense. Originally purchased in 1911 by a famous American jockey named Tod Sloan, the bar soon passed to former bartender Harry MacElhone, who lent it his name and gave it the sort of New York flair likely to attract American clientele.

Like Bar Hemingway, Harry's New York Bar was a popular haunt for the celebrities of the day, including Humphrey Bogart, Jack Dempsey, Sinclair Lewis, and, of course, Ernest Hemingway. It wasn't just popular among Americans, either: celebrities from around the world, such as Coco Chanel and Prince Serge Obolensky were known patrons. Even James Bond visited the hotel—in Ian Fleming's novel *A View to Kill*.

Why You Should Drink Your Martini Here: Setting aside its incredible list of regulars, Harry's New York Bar is a fascinating look into the rise of martini culture. Visiting Harry's, it isn't hard to see how American expatriates might be drawn to the place. In fact, the bar today caters more to tourists than to locals, going so far as to serve hot dogs. It's a fascinating bar that feels almost out of place in Paris—but also makes you feel right at home.

CHARLIE PALMER AT THE KNICK, NEW YORK CITY

Name: Charlie Palmer at the Knick
Location: Knickerbocker Hotel, New York City, New York, USA
Founded: 2015
Website: theknickerbocker.com

Cultural Significance: The Knickerbocker Hotel has made multiple appearances in this book, with good reason. Many consider the hotel to be the birthplace of the martini, and while the hotel and its drinking establishments have undergone considerable change since the early 1900s, Charlie Palmer at the Knick is the current home of the Knickerbocker Martini, an elegant homage to the famous cocktail and its origins.

Charlie Palmer at the Knick may not have been around when the martini was first being served to Rockefeller, Bogart, or Frank Sinatra, but the establishment has not shied away from the hotel's illustrious history. The Knickerbocker Martini features elements from the classic recipe, with the sort of modern twist the bar has become known for.

Why You Should Drink Your Martini Here: Charlie Palmer at the Knick offers the perfect combination of old school and new school. The Knickerbocker Hotel's place in martini history is assured, but Charlie Palmer has a chance to add to it, despite being a relative newcomer. Offering all the amenities that you might expect from a modern martini bar and an austere, historic backdrop, this is the perfect place to appreciate both where the martini came from and where it is headed.

THE MARTINI BAR, CAPE TOWN

Name: The Martini Bar at Cellars-Hohenort Hotel
Location: Cellars-Hohenort Hotel, Cape Town, South Africa
Founded: 1993
Website: thecellars-hohenorthotel.com

Cultural Significance: As with Origin in Hong Kong, The Martini Bar within the Cellars-Hohenort Hotel in Cape Town, South Africa, serves as proof that the martini can be properly respected outside of North America and Europe. The owners of hotel so revered the cocktail that they could think of no more fitting name for their bar—thus, The Martini Bar was born.

The hotel website features a blog suggesting different martini variants (as well as other cocktails), inviting guests and non-guests alike to sample the expertly crafted drinks invented by their talented mixologists. In addition to martini variations, The Martini Bar offers craft coffee and a considerable wine list, emphasizing their dedication to the beauty of simplicity.

Why You Should Drink Your Martini Here: You might not expect the martini to be popular in Africa, but The Martini Bar seeks to dissuade you of that misconception. The decor within The Martini Bar is both tasteful and elegant, a true reflection of its namesake, and the bartenders are capable of mixing a classic dry martini or composing a delicious variant you might never have thought possible.

GIN PALACE, MELBOURNE

Name: Gin Palace
Location: Melbourne, Australia
Founded: 1997
Website: ginpalace.com.au

Cultural Significance: In the early days of gin, the term "gin palace" was used as a pejorative. Rather than run from that history, this Australian establishment has elected to lean into it, embracing the term's royal implications and turning what might once have been an insult into the highest of compliments.

In fact, Gin Palace is named after an old speakeasy in Melbourne, an establishment that rose to prominence under that very name. Although that establishment was shut down, its spirit lives on in today's Gin Palace, an establishment whose owners strive to capture the welcoming atmosphere and rebellious attitude of its namesake. Gin Palace prides itself on serving guests around the clock while creating a feeling of class and dignity.

Why You Should Drink Your Martini Here: At Gin Palace, it is, as you might expect, all about the gin. The establishment features an extensive martini menu, and you'll find a staff well versed in not just the flavor of gin, but its history. Gin Palace is also famous for its raucous parties, and the legends of its fifth and 10th anniversaries echo to this day. You simply won't find a more perfect place to enjoy a martini in Australia.

REFERENCES

bmj.com/content/319/7225/1600.full

liquor.com/articles/behind-the-drink-the-martini

sipsmith.com/our-story/gin-history

thrillist.com/drink/nation/understanding-vermouth-history-of-vermouth

drymartiniorg.com/historia-origenes-vermut/?lang=en

tanqueray.com

bombaysapphire.com

beefeatergin.com

us.hendricksgin.com

plymouthgin.com

martini.com

noillyprat.com

gallo.com

imbuecellars.com

thelocal.fr/20140822/when-hemingway-took-back-the-ritz-bar

dukeshotel.com

21club.com

ritzparis.com

originbar.hk

harrysbar.fr

thecellars-hohenorthotel.com

martinimuse.com/how_the_martini_got_its_name.shtml

afi.com/100years/quotes.aspx

dummies.com/food-drink/drinks/spirits/getting-to-know-london-dry-gins

sfgate.com/wine/article/The-Truth-About-Vermouth-3273102.php

10best.com/awards/travel/best-craft-gin-distillery-2017

hardshoredistilling.com

staugustinedistillery.com

newhollandbrew.com

stgeorgespirits.com

leopoldbros.com

ginpalace.com.au

threeclubs.com

npr.org/sections/thesalt/2012/10/05/162305178/shake-it-up-baby-are-martinis-made-the-bond-way-better

chemistryworld.com/feature/shaken-not-stirred/3004781.article

gastropod.com/the-cocktail-hour

www.noorbar.com

theknickerbocker.com

PHOTO CREDITS

8: Courtesy of Movie Poster Image Art/Getty Images

9: *The Bar-tender's Guide; or How to Mix All Kinds of Plain and Fancy Drinks*. Jerry Thomas (New York: Dick & Fitzgerald), 1887. Courtesy of the Library of Congress

10-11: BMI/ Shutterstock.com

12: Courtesy of the Wellcome Collection, London

16: Mary Evans Picture Library/Everett Collection

148: Photo by Jason Wong on Unsplash

150-151: Courtesy of Tanqueray

157: Courtesy of Leopold Bros.

158-159: Courtesy of Hardshore Distilling; martini photo by Jordan Milne and bottle photo by Anthony Di Biase.

162-163: Courtesy of St. George Spirits

164: Courtesy of Maison Noilly Prat

171: Courtesy of Quady Winery

172-173, 178: Courtesy of 21 Club

183: Courtesy of The Ritz Hotel, Paris

184, 187: Courtesy of Tasting Groups Limited

190: Courtesy of The Cellars-Hohenort, Cape Town

193: Courtesy of Gin Palace, Melbourne

All other images are used under official license from Shutterstock.com

ABOUT THE AUTHOR

SHANE CARLEY, a longtime aficionado of all types of alcohol, jumped at the opportunity to launch a series of cocktail books. *The Martini Field Guide* follows previous publications including *The Mason Jar Cocktail Companion*, *The Home Bartender*, and *Red Cup Nation*. By day, he works as a content developer for a New Hampshire university. Weekends, however, are spent on serious book research.

ABOUT CIDER MILL PRESS BOOK PUBLISHERS

Good ideas ripen with time. From seed to harvest, Cider Mill Press brings fine reading, information, and entertainment together between the covers of its creatively crafted books. Our Cider Mill bears fruit twice a year, publishing a new crop of titles each spring and fall.

"Where Good Books Are Ready for Press"

501 Nelson Place
Nashville, Tennessee 37214

cidermillpress.com